I0793927

The WINDOWS OF HIS HEART

I thought he was trying to open the windows of his heart to me, and at the same time endeavoring to read my disposition and character.

—GENERAL OLIVER O. HOWARD, SPRING 1875

The WINDOWS OF HIS HEART

CHIEF JOSEPH OF THE NEZ PERCE

LOUISE LENAHAN WALLACE

PLAIN SIGHT PUBLISHING
An imprint of Cedar Fort, Inc.
Springville, Utah

Paperback ISBN 13: 978-1-4621-4991-9
eBook ISBN 13: 978-1-4621-4992-6

Published by Plain Sight Publishing, an imprint of Cedar Fort, Inc.
2373 W. 700 S., Suite 100, Springville, UT 84663
Distributed by Cedar Fort, Inc., www.cedarfort.com

Library of Congress Control Number: 2025938889

Cover design by Shawnda Craig

Printed in the United States of America

10 9 8 7 6 5 4 3 2 1

Printed on acid-free paper

To Aunt Marny and Uncle Bill Caldwell.
Thank you for being there.
With love from your Prolly

CONTENTS

AUTHOR'S NOTE

When one writes about the life of an individual who is over a century dead, it is probable there are no living witnesses to confirm indubitably that a particular action, speech, or event took place in a particular way at a particular time. One treading the biographical waters of a personage who has not been alive for 120 years must, perforce, rely upon written records and accounts handed down through the spoken word. It then follows that the aspiring biographer must also rely upon memory of a situation passed down through the generations.

Both methods have their drawbacks.

The written word, if presently considered a reliable record, at the time of writing was colored by the author's perceptions of the situation, or those of the person who gave him the information. Similarly, the spoken record acquires vagaries of "fact" in repetition from generation to generation and speaker to listener to speaker—rather like the childhood game Telephone during which several players sit in a circle and the leader whispers a sentence in the ear of the person seated beside her. That person passes on *what she heard* to the next player and so around the circle until the last participant speaks aloud what he heard passed on to him. Inevitably, the final version is vastly changed from the original and may actually present a negative quality, even though the first sentence was positive and cheerful.

Thus it has been in my search for the truth about Chief Joseph, the Nez Perce, and the United States Army. I relied upon earliest records gleaned from eyewitness accounts. The next reviewers sifted this information and produced their honestly given, but nevertheless personally colored, viewpoints. The following generation gave their interpretation of "what really happened"—and so it continued to the present. A case in point, albeit a minor one, is Chief Joseph's Nez Perce's name. It has been given variously as In-mut-too-yah-lat-lat (Thunder Traveling over the Mountains); Hinmaton Yalatkit (Thunder Rolling in the Heights); and Hin-mah-too-yah-lat-kekht (Thunder Traveling to Loftier Mountain Heights).

Current reports belie many of the early "facts." Those earlier interpretations, accepted as historically accurate for many years, are now being challenged by the new generation of researchers. In some instances, the circumstances are bluntly pointed out as "ridiculous" and "impossible to have occurred." Right or wrong? Fair or unjust? No one now alive can truly know the details of those events of more than 145 years ago.

I have researched extensively. In instances of conflicting "facts," I searched until I found three documented versions of the incident. I then accepted as "truth" the two versions that agreed. If I found only two versions and they disagreed, I did not include them without so specifying the conflicting viewpoints.

Memories and written records are not infallible. Neither are painstakingly-careful-with-the-facts biographers. It is with this knowledge that I present this work.

PROLOGUE

During the Nez Perce flight to Canada in 1877, Chief Joseph conducted the most scientific campaign ever commanded by an Indian against the United States Army. No one knew better than he the tremendous odds against him, yet, for the freedom of his people, he fought with a force of never more than three hundred warriors against a total of two thousand soldiers at various times. He opposed in battle veteran troops of the Civil War, considered the greatest soldiers in the world. He earned ungrudging praise from those same soldiers and from ordinary citizens across the United States. How was he able to achieve such high personal recognition in the face of such profound adversity?

Joseph, Chief of the Nez Perce Indians from 1871 to 1904, has been termed one of the "most romantic and important figures in the history of the Pacific Northwest."[1] He is principally noted for being the reluctant but highly effective leader of the Nez Perce uprising of 1877, and for this feat, the nickname Indian Napoleon was bestowed upon him.[2]

Chief Joseph's forebears had lived in Oregon's Grande Ronde River country. The Wallowa Mountains, and Wallowa Lake in their midst, are in the northeast corner of Oregon. The Treaty of 1855 gave the Nez Perce an area extending from the Clearwater River, which crosses the Washington–Idaho border, south through the Wallowa and Imnaha regions of present-day Oregon and Idaho. The Upper Nez Perce, of whom Lawyer was a prominent chief, lived in Idaho on a branch of the Clearwater near Lapwai (Place Where the Butterfly Dwells)[3]; the lower Nez Perce, with Tu-eka-kas—Old Chief Joseph—and Looking Glass as honored leaders, lived further south around the Wallowa and Imnaha Valleys.

In 1860 the discovery of gold in the Clearwater–Salmon area brought prospectors from Walla Walla to the gold fields. As they crossed the fertile Wallowa Valley, they realized it was excellent farmland and began settling there, in spite of the stipulation of the Treaty of 1855 that no white person could claim land on a reservation. The Lower Nez Perce protested this invasion, but by 1863, so many whites had taken up land there that the government decided the settlers couldn't be removed, so it ordered a new treaty. The Treaty of 1863 limited the Nez Perce to the region around Lapwai. Lower Nez Perce Tu-eka-kas refused to sign the new treaty, although Chief Lawyer and several other Nez Perce did so. Lawyer had few qualms about signing; the ancestral lands of his band were within the circumference of the newly shrunken reservation.

Because of this geographical accident and Lawyer's readiness to sign, the whites unilaterally decided he was chief of all the Nez Perce. When they obtained his signature, the whites decided that all the Nez Perce were bound by his agreement to move to the Lapwai country in Idaho.[4] This signing created a serious difference of opinion—the whites considered the signatures received to be binding on all the Nez Perce; the Lower Nez Perce, who had not signed, considered the Treaty non-existent and ignored it, while striving to prevent white settlers from claiming any more land in the Lapwai region.

In the early days of their association with the Nez Perce, French–Canadian trappers referred to them as "Pierced Noses" because some wore shell ornaments in their noses.[5] Chief Joseph's ancestors, peace-loving cousins of the Idaho Nez Perce, lived in harmony with the white man and gained the reputation of never having been known to slay a white, in spite of such obstacles as the Treaties of 1855 and 1863. In spite of the refusal of Tu-eka-kas and his followers, who were living in Oregon, to sign the Treaty and move to the Lapwai Reservation, the government did not enforce this dictum for the next thirteen years.[6]

In 1873, a conference took place in Idaho at Lapwai between various Indian chiefs and government officials. In the spirit of his father before him, Young Chief Joseph refused to move to the reservation in Idaho or to the Umatilla Reservation in eastern Oregon. This refusal was duly reported to the Secretary of the Interior, who decreed that the Nez Perce could remain in the Wallowa area—the "valley of winding waters"[7]—during the next summer and fall. By Presidential order, the Wallowa and Imnaha Valleys were designated for Chief Joseph and the non-treaty Indians.

In January 1877, when conflict between the Wallowa Nez Perce and the white settlers escalated, the federal government ordered General Oliver Howard to remove all the Nez Perce to the Lapwai area, the area set aside in the 1863 Treaty as their reservation.[8]

In May 1877, General Howard informed Chief Joseph that if "his people" were not on the reservation in thirty days, all the cattle and livestock outside the reservation would fall to the whites. If Howard had allowed them reasonable time to complete their preparations, events might have proceeded without violence because Chief Joseph had already convinced his people to go.

Joseph's people believed in him—enough to follow him for seventy-five days, across eighteen hundred miles, battling the while against the most terrible obstacles. Why did they do it? *How* did he do it?

Ralph Stogdill's *Handbook of Leadership: A Survey of Theory and Research*[9] provides insight into Chief Joseph's character during that journey. Stogdill was for many years Associate Director of the Ohio State Leadership Studies, and Management Director of the Academy of Management. When the Smith Richardson Foundation asked him to provide an analysis and review of the literature on leadership, he defined his assignment as "that of assembling all the published evidence on a given topic and summarizing the findings."[10] He notes that leadership is defined as the initiation and maintenance of structure in expectations and interaction. Included in Stogdill's profile listing of attributes indispensable for a "true" leader are such traits as 1) role retention, 2) persuasiveness, 3) demand reconciliation, 4) influence with superiors, 5) initiation of structure, 6) integration, 7) production emphasis, 8) predictive accuracy, 9) tolerance of freedom, 10) consideration, 11) tolerance of uncertainty, and 12) representation.[11]

The study of leadership is an ancient art, reaching back to Plato, Caesar, and Plutarch. The early Egyptians believed their king possessed three divine qualities, summed up thus: "Authoritative utterance is in thy mouth, perception is in thy heart, and thy tongue is the shrine of justice."[12] The *Funk & Wagnalls New Standard Dictionary of the English Language* defines *leader* as

> one who leads . . . one who occupies a chief or prominent place; especially, one fitted by force of ideas, character . . . or by strength of will . . . to direct men in conduct and achievement.[13]

This same dictionary explains leadership as "ability to lead, guidance."[14]

Stogdill's *Handbook of Leadership* notes that leadership is a universal human phenomenon. He defines leadership as "the initiation and maintenance of structure in expectation and interaction."[15] But the *qualities* of leadership regarded as important to one culture, society, or generation may not be so considered by another group in another time or place. If Stogdill's attributes profile a leader of the late twentieth and early twenty-first centuries, how closely do they characterize a leader of the late nineteenth and early twentieth centuries—an individual separated from our present day not only by the time span of 120 years since his death, but also by twelve decades of shifting social values, cultural structures, and ethnic mores?

A study of Chief Joseph (In-mut-too-yah-lat-lat—Thunder-Traveling-Over-the-Mountains)[16] explores this concept.

1

ROLE RETENTION

Actively exercises leadership role rather than surrendering leadership to others

The earth and myself are of one mind.[17]

Arguments have arisen concerning whether Joseph was the actual war chief of the 1877 campaign or whether he was camp guardian—protector of the women, children, and old men. Josephy says:

> He had inherited his father's tolerance, compassion, and gentle manner and was a civil, rather than a hunting or military chief. He carried himself with dignity, could speak with eloquence and logic, and was already known among the non-treaties as a man of wisdom and peace.[18]

Beal, in *I Will Fight No More Forever*, points out:

> The military officers assumed that Joseph was the dominant chieftain. Lieutenant Wood, General Howard's aide, made the most positive statement upon this point by writing, "He (Joseph) was, in council, at first probably not so influential as White Bird and the group of chiefs that sustained him, but from first to last he (Joseph) was preeminently their war chief. Such was the testimony of his followers after the surrender, and such seems to be the evidence of the campaign itself."[19]

Nez Perce Country: A Handbook for the National Park says:

> Joseph's stature as a non-treaty spokesman and diplomat had loomed so large before the war that Howard and the newspaper writers with him readily assumed he was leading the non-treaties and was responsible for such shrewd tactics as those that had just led the army on a difficult and fruitless chase. As the non-treaties continued to outmaneuver and frustrate the army, the assumption became firmer, and Joseph's reputation as a military genius grew until the entire conflict became known, undeservedly as it was, as "Chief Joseph's War."[20]

This distinction between war chief and camp guardian is drawn with a fine line when considering Joseph's qualities as a leader. His was a "sacred trust."[21] He fought only in self-defense when the families of the five bands involved in the retreat were hard-pressed by the soldiers.[22]

On October 3, 1876, Zachary Chandler, Secretary of the Interior, appointed a commission to meet with the Nez Perce at Lapwai, Idaho, to try to settle their differences. Among the commissioners he named for the November 1876 council were General Oliver O. Howard and Major Henry Clay Wood. Chief Joseph, exhibiting his sense of independence by traveling at his own pace, delayed the start of the meeting for almost a week. Scouts reported him on his way, but he simply refused to hurry, "official orders" notwithstanding. A few miles from the Lapwai Agency, he made camp for the night. When the commission's chairman and interpreter visited him there and strongly suggested he hurry, he replied that "his business even now, did not demand haste."[23]

He knew the commission couldn't begin without him, and he took full advantage of the knowledge to emphasize that his presence there was as an equal of the government committee and not as an underling obeying the command of his rulers.

After he had delayed the start of the meeting for almost a week, he arrived at the council grounds, ready to begin the discussions. He was extremely courteous and polite, dignified, agreeable, pleasantly conforming to the best diplomatic standards, willing to exchange endless compliments and light conversation with the officials, but when the question of the Wallowa was broached, he would not budge from his previous position; he would not compromise, he would not submit to white authority. To any and all proposals, he politely, firmly responded, "No."[24]

At one point, Chief Joseph stood and broached a topic the commissioners had neglected: a man's unwillingness to be driven from his home. The Commissioner's Report recorded his words:

> The Creative Power, when he made the earth, made no marks, no lines of division or separation on it. The earth was his mother. He was made of the earth and grew up on its bosom. The earth, as his mother and nurse, was sacred to his affections, too sacred to be valued by or sold for silver and gold. He could not consent to sever his affections from the land that bore him. He asked nothing of the President. He was able to take care of himself.[25]

The commissioners, dignified in their representation of the United States Government, could not resent his polite defiance, which inability undoubtedly exasperated them no end.

When asked by the commissioners about the differences between the non-treaty and treaty Nez Perce, Chief Joseph told them, "At the time the 1855 treaty was made, we divided. The treaty was the cause of it. From that time we have been separated. We still remain so."[26]

General Howard wrote that "Indian Joseph and his malcontents denied the jurisdiction of the United States over them. They were offered everything they wanted, if they would simply submit to the authority and government of the United States agents."[27]

Chief Joseph had, apparently, three main reasons for refusing to give in to the commissioners: 1) He firmly believed his people owned the disputed land. 2) His deep-set independence refused to allow himself or his people to be controlled by a "foreign" government. 3) From past experience, he strongly distrusted that government to keep its promise. In addition, he had no reason to believe that if his people moved to Lapwai, the land would be permanently theirs. Twice since the Treaty of 1855, the reservation had been reduced in size. The Wallowa Valley had been sold by the treaty faction in 1863. Perhaps most telling of all, Chief Joseph had learned through bitter experience that the government's use of the phrase *permanent home* had two connotations: one for promises and one for actuality. Only when he believed he had succeeded in getting his point across to the commission, Joseph returned to Wallowa.[28]

In May 1877, General Howard invited Chiefs Joseph, Looking Glass, and White Bird to ride with him to find suitable land for the Nez Perce. As they traversed rich, rolling countryside inhabited by both white settlers and Indians, Howard suggested that if Chief Joseph wanted this land, he (Howard) would evict the Indians and whites and give the land to the Nez Perce. Chief Joseph replied, "No. It would be wrong to disturb these people. I have no right to take their homes. I have never taken what did not belong to me. I will not now."[29] They were unable to find any suitable unoccupied land, and the next day, General Howard issued his ultimatum that the Nez Perce had thirty days to move to the Lapwai Reservation or the Army would remove them by force.

The Indians "realized they would either have to move to the reservation or fight. Again the chiefs, obedient to Chief Joseph's wishes, decided in favor of peace and manifested an air of friendliness, but rancor blazed in their hearts."[30]

Long-simmering tempers finally boiled when President Ulysses S. Grant abruptly ordered all the Nez Perce to report immediately to the Lapwai Reservation. The result, Chief Joseph's War, was one of the five major Indian wars that occurred in the Pacific Northwest between 1847 and 1877.[31]

Various reasons have been set out for President Grant's actions in the spring of 1877. One of the most probable is the pressure put on Grant by white squatters who decided they wanted the Indian lands and that President Grant was the one to obtain them. In the ensuing weeks, squatters committed outrages on the Nez Perce, who retaliated by killing twenty whites. The issue thus forced, Chief Joseph made his decision to escape to Canada with two hundred warriors and six hundred women and children.[32]

2
PERSUASIVENESS
Uses persuasion and argument effectively; exhibits strong convictions

---

I claim a right to live on my land, and accord you the privilege to live on yours.[33]

In 1805, the Lewis and Clark expedition met the Nez Perce on the Weippe prairie in what is now northern Idaho. The father of Red Grizzly Bear confirmed that the Nez Perce were convinced of the advantages of peace and ardently wished to cultivate peace with their neighbors. He concluded with the promise that the "whitemen" might be assured of their warmest attachment and that they would always give them every assistance in their power; that they were poor but their hearts were good. This council and the Nez Perce promise of friendship and alliance with the Americans had an enduring significance. Word of the agreement was spread among the villages, and knowledge was passed from generation to generation that the Nez Perce leaders had given their word to Lewis and Clark. The Nez Perce saw to it that the younger people understood the promise given in the Kamiah Valley and honored it.

This was why, speaking of this meeting many years later, Chief Joseph was able to say:

> All the Nez Perces made friends with Lewis and Clark, and agreed to let them pass through their country, and never to

> make war on white men. This promise the Nez Perces have never broken. No white man can accuse them of bad faith, and speak with a straight tongue.[34]

When the Wallowa Valley was ceded to the United States Government by the Treaty of June 9, 1863, the act was "without legal right."[35] Chief Joseph's attitude was one of quiet strength and dignity. He felt no awe of any man, red or white, and owed none of them allegiance.

Hence he could ignore orders from government officials and the president with a clear conscience.[36] If anyone offered him arguments, threats, or orders, he merely said no, he did not agree; no, he was not afraid; no, he would not obey. He did not feel bound to the Treaty of 1863 because he believed "the old Treaty has never been correctly reported."[37]

Joseph offered the argument:

> If we ever owned the land, we own it still, for we have never sold it. In the treaty councils the commissioners have claimed that our country had been sold to the government. Suppose a white man should come to me and say, "Joseph, I like your horses and I want to buy them." I say to him, "No, my horses suit me, I will not sell them." Then he goes to my neighbor, and says to him: "Joseph has some good horses. I want to buy them but he refuses to sell." My neighbor answers, "Pay me the money and I will sell you Joseph's horses." The white man returns to me and says, "Joseph, I have bought your horses, and you must let me have them." If we sold our lands to the government, this is the way they were bought.[38]

John B. Monteith, the Lapwai Reservation Agent, asked Chief Joseph if the Nez Perce intended to drive out the white settlers. Chief Joseph again explained that the Wallowa belonged to his people and insisted that the whites must leave. Monteith argued that the country was sold to the government, that it had been surveyed and put on the market, and that the government would protect the settlers. Joseph told him that it was a lie to say that his father had sold the valley.[39]

In March 1873, the Commissioner of Indian Affairs appointed a three-man group to investigate the condition of the Indian tribes in Idaho and adjacent territories. Thus Chief Joseph met at Lapwai with Monteith and T. B. Odeneal, Superintendent of Indian Affairs for Oregon.

After lengthy discussion, Monteith and Odeneal concluded that Chief Joseph had the right of the matter on his side. The white settlers, used to the mild climate of the Willamette Valley, were surprised and discouraged when early frost hit their wheat fields and house gardens, indicating that the Wallowa Valley land was too high and cold to farm but satisfactory for the hunting, fishing, and stock raising the Nez Perce carried on.

Monteith's report to the Commissioner of Indian Affairs included his opinion:

> If there is any way in which the Wallowa Valley could be kept for the Indians I would recommend that it be done. There is not one house in the valley so far as I could ascertain but some will be built this fall. The question will have to be settled soon to those Indians living outside the Reserve.[40]

Monteith and Odeneal recommended to President Grant that the entire area of the upper Wallowa Valley and Wallowa Lake be set aside permanently as a hunting preserve for the Nez Perce. Their recommendations included the provision that the white settlers should be removed from the valley, with the government paying them for improvements they had made to their land, and the area then closed to white settlement. The Indian Bureau approved this report.

On June 16, 1873, President Grant signed an order that set aside a portion of the Wallowa Valley for a hunting reserve. Unfortunately, this order did not include the same area discussed by Odeneal and Monteith in their report. Monteith and Odeneal had recommended Chief Joseph be given a portion which included high ground, Wallowa Lake, and the headwaters of the Wallowa and Imnaha Rivers. He was given the northern portion but not the upper part of the Wallowa Valley containing Old Chief Joseph's grave.

Monteith began urging Joseph to settle down and farm, but "they said they did not want the [Wallowa] valley for farming purposes but for that of hunting and fishing. I replied that that was not sufficient, that the Government expected more of them. Still they refused."[41]

At this point Monteith's attitude toward the Nez Perce showed definite change; he became stubborn and demanding. He simply could not accept that they wanted to hunt, fish, and raise horses instead of farm. He also closed his mind to the fact that farming was against their religion. He wrote to the commissioner of Indian Affairs:

> I am of the opinion that Joseph and his band are not entitled to the Wallowa unless they go there and settle down. . . . I would ask what course I shall take in case Joseph attempts to create a disturbance.[42]

The new reservation included the lower Wallowa, the right bank of the lower Grande Ronde, and a plateau between the Grande Ronde and the Snake River. Consequently, the Nez Perce received a large area of pine-forested land unsuitable for farming, while the land along the Wallowa River remained open to farming. The only way for the whites to reach this land, however, was to cross the new reservation. Because Chief Joseph and his people claimed the entire Wallowa Valley, they were understandably upset to retain only half of it.

A custom prevailed by which several Indians each year were allowed to go to the Indian Bureau in Washington, DC to discuss problems with the top officials in the Bureau. Chief Joseph requested to be part of this delegation, but Monteith arbitrarily denied his request.[43]

In November 1875, two Catholic priests were assigned to the Nez Perce mission. They intended to build a school and a house for themselves. At this point, Monteith, as the Lapwai Reservation Agent, decreed that they could build a church and a house but no school. As the construction progressed, Monteith became convinced the priests were building a larger than necessary house that could include the forbidden school. The Nez Perce were amused by this opposition between the Indian Agent and the Catholic priests. The non-treaty Nez Perce were most vocal about the weakness that such a government and such a religion obviously contained.

The Presbyterians began to fear that the Catholics would wean the Nez Perce away from the Protestant faith, and one of the commissioners asked Chief Joseph:

> "Do you want schools or school houses on the Wallowa Reservation?"
>
> "No," he had answered. "We do not want schools or school houses on the Wallowa Reservation."
>
> "Why do you not want schools?"
>
> "They will teach us to have churches."
>
> "Do you not want churches?"
>
> "No, we do not want churches."
>
> "Why do you not want churches?"
>
> "They will teach us," Joseph said, "to quarrel about God, as the Catholics and Protestants do on the Nez Perce Reservation and at other places. We may quarrel with men sometimes about things on this earth, but we never quarrel about God. We do not want to learn that."[44]

Monteith became furious when Chief Joseph commented on such religious quarrels—he knew only too well Chief Joseph was referring to the fight between the priests and the Indian Agent.[45]

Of his spiritual training, Chief Joseph said:

> Our fathers gave us many laws, which they had learned from their fathers. These laws were good. They told us to treat all men as they treated us; that we should never be the first to break a bargain; that it was a disgrace to tell a lie; that we should speak only the truth; that it was a shame for one man to take from another his wife, or his property without paying for it. We were taught to believe that the Great Spirit sees and hears everything, and that he never forgets; that hereafter he will give every man a spirit-home

> according to his deserts [*sic*]; if he has been a good man, he will have a good home; if he has been a bad man, he will have a bad home. This I believe and all my people believe the same.[46]

At the November 1876 council at Lapwai, concerning whether the Nez Perce should give up their claim to the Wallowa Valley in Oregon, Chief Joseph said, "Never relinquish the claim to the land. No band had any right to sell land belonging to another band. Their different tracts were like counties making up a state, but a state cannot sell its counties."[47]

At the May 1877 council, the non-treaty Nez Perce heard talk that their religious rights were to be prohibited. Chief Joseph replied thus:

> I am ready to talk today. I have been in a great many councils, but I am no wiser. We are all sprung from a woman, although we are unlike in many things. We cannot be made over again. You are as you were made, and as you were made you can remain. We are just as we were made by the Great Spirit, and you cannot change us; then why should children of one mother and one father quarrel—why should one try to cheat the other? I do not believe that the Great Spirit Chief gave one kind of men the right to tell another kind of men what they must do.[48]

Chief Joseph also stated: "We are not to be trampled upon and our rights taken from us. The right to the land was ours before the whites came among us."[49]

Perhaps some of the difficulties between the Indians and the white settlers evolved because of differences in concept. To the white man, "home" was a permanent building on land that he did not leave, where he remained with his family and carried on his work of farming, stock tending and living. The Indian "home" was different portions of land used in different seasons. When the Indian changed land portions, he took his family and his "house" with him. Neither the white man nor the Indian could accept the other's way of life as "normal." This philosophy caused white politicians to accuse the Indians of having a roving nature and no desire to live in fixed housing.[50]

In this vein, under pressure from white settlers, Leonard Grover, governor of Oregon, complained to President Grant that Chief Joseph, because he traveled from area to area instead of living in one place year round, had lost any claim to the Wallowa Valley.

Howard's earliest actions hint that he personally felt Chief Joseph and his band should be allowed to live permanently on the Wallowa Reservation. He wrote:

> I think it a great mistake to take from Joseph and his band of Nez Perce Indians that valley. The white people really do not want it . . . possibly Congress can be induced to let these really peaceable Indians have this poor valley for their own.[51]

Ultimately, however, his military orders prevailed over any private feelings. In spite of Joseph's efforts, the government commission ruled in favor of the settlers. The Nez Perce were given General Howard's ultimatum to move out.[52]

Many farmers who had believed the land would be returned to the Nez Perce expressed deep disappointment at the commission's ruling—they had been holding on to their land, expecting that they could sell it to the government for a tidy profit.

When the Nez Perce War of 1877 began, unfounded rumors spread over the countryside. At Palouse City, two hundred settlers jammed into a stockade to defend themselves. At Colfax, the whites crowded into their schoolhouse. At Penawawa, a makeshift "fort" which included gunports was constructed of bales of wool that had been waiting for shipment. In spite of the panic, no Indian depredations occurred.

On May 18, 1873, the Wallowa *Sentinel* published the following piece by a Wallowa resident:

> As regards the contemplated Indian troubles, I know nothing but hearsay, which is worth less than nothing. . . . I do not think there is much danger of the Indians committing any

> depredation, notwithstanding all that the Indian agents and superintendents can do to urge the Indians to break out. It is my honest opinion that a majority of the Indian agents steal the goods that the government justly allows red men and then encourages the Indians to murder the settlers.[53]

In response to the "sensible solution" that part of the valley be set aside for the Indians and that white settlers be prohibited from entering or settling said part, the editor of the *Sentinel* "shrieked in print":

> Those of the people who have not heard the news . . . giving the Wallowa Valley to the Indians, will almost be struck dumb with the intelligence. . . . There have been many perfidious officials in Oregon, but the man Odeneal, Superintendent of Indian Affairs, stinks in the nostrils of every decent man east of the Cascades, for the dirty part he has acted in robbing the settlers of the Wallowa of their homes. . . . We now propose that the whites be put on a reservation and closely guarded so that they may inflict no damage on the noble red men![54]

Chief Joseph definitely expressed persuasiveness and strong convictions about his family. The Nez Perce practiced polygamy and after Chief Joseph's first wife died, he married two widows of slain Nez Perce warriors. When a missionary tried to persuade him to give up one, Chief Joseph replied, "I fought all through the war for my country and these women. You took away my country; I shall keep my wives."[55]

3

DEMAND RECONCILIATION

Reconciles conflicting organizational demands and reduces disorder to system

---

Lieutenant Forse reported that "Joseph could have fallen upon the settlers in detail, killing them and destroying their property."[56]

In April 1876, two settlers, Wells McNall and A. B. Findley, entered a Nez Perce camp and accused Wil-hau-tyah, one of the braves, of stealing their horses. The Indian denied the charge. McNall grabbed him. He defended himself. Findley shot him. The men later found their horses, but even though Lapwai Reservation Agent John B. Monteith reported the shooting as "willful, deliberate murder,"[57] nothing was done to assuage the Nez Perce, and tension mounted.

General Howard was deeply concerned about the danger of a new Indian war. He was a strongly religious and moralistic man and was particularly moved by a letter from the Reverend A. L. Lindsley, who wrote:

> Joseph's band's title has never been rightfully extinguished. In fact the fair construction of treaty stipulations confirms the Indian title. The Treaty of 1863 was not adopted by the Nez Perce tribe but by a part only. The Government is bound by its own engagement to fulfill the original Treaty of 1855, until it can procure an honorable discharge from its obligations.[58]

In July 1876, after the Findley–McNall episode, a meeting took place at Lapwai between Major Henry C. Wood, other military officers, Chief Joseph, and some forty members of the Wallowa band. Chief Joseph said the Indian who had been killed was a quiet, peaceable man. The whites who had killed him were the aggressors and he (Chief Joseph) wished the white who had done the killing to be brought to the agency to face his accusers. Chief Joseph pointed out that among the Indians the chiefs controlled the members of their bands, with power to prevent bad Indians from doing wicked things and in case of their doing so to punish them. If the chiefs did not restrain or punish bad Indians, they themselves were responsible for their acts. He reasoned that those in authority over the whites had or should have the same control over their men. Thus, the white authorities in the vicinity of Wallowa Valley and elsewhere were directly responsible for the killing of his brother.[59] Wood and the other officers showed their sympathy and respect for Joseph. Howard asked that another commission be appointed to "settle the whole matter before war is even thought of."[60]

In August 1876, Chief Joseph and forty-five lodges of his band met with Captain Whipple in council. Captain Whipple told the Nez Perce that the Army was present as friends of both Indians and whites, as long as each tried to do right, and that the settlers had informed him they did not object to the Indians coming into the valley if they would observe the laws and do no violence to persons or property. In his report, Whipple wrote that "Joseph replied at considerable length acknowledging the justice of my requirements and promised observance."[61]

In September 1876, white and Indian emotions intensified because of the Findley–McNall episode. When a council consisting of Chief Joseph's band and a group of settlers failed to resolve the dispute, the Indians lost patience and ordered the settlers to be out of the valley by the following Sunday. At this point, the Army, in the person of Lieutenant Albert Forse, Commander of Fort Walla Walla, arrived with his troops to persuade Chief Joseph and his band to back off from their demands.

Forse and Chief Joseph met alone on top of a hill and discussed the situation. Chief Joseph told Forse that the cause of the trouble was the killing of Wil-hau-tyah by McNall and Findley, but the Nez Perce would concede if a white man's court would try McNall and Findley in a fair manner. When Forse asked Chief Joseph about the threats to the settlers, Chief Joseph responded that the settlers had bragged that they intended to kill and scalp Chief Joseph and his followers. When Forse questioned Chief Joseph's refusal to go to the Lapwai reservation, Chief Joseph said that he had discussed the matter with Major Wood and that a Washington commission was to decide the outcome. Realizing that he might be interfering in an agreement between Chief Joseph and the government, Forse didn't pursue the question. Rather, he suggested that Chief Joseph keep his horses and people near the lake, away from the settlers, and named Hurricane Creek as the boundary line beyond which the Indians should not pass except to go to the Grande Ronde for supplies, and then only two braves at a time. Chief Joseph agreed to all this, "and to show his good faith he would throw away the bullets they had put in their guns for the purpose of killing the Whites, who had come to kill him. He did this by forming his Indians in a single rank, and discharging their pieces."[62]

In 1871, Chief Joseph's father died. Before his death, he told Joseph:

> My son, my body is returning to my mother earth, and my spirit is going very soon to see the Great Spirit Chief. When I am gone, think of your country. You are the chief of these people. They look to you to guide them. Always remember that your father never sold his country. This country holds your father's body. Never sell the bones of your father and mother.

"I buried him in that beautiful valley of the winding waters," Joseph said years later. "I love that land more than all the rest in the world. A man who would not love his father's grave is worse than a wild animal."[63]

In January 1877, when conflict between the Wallowa Nez Perce and the white settlers escalated, the federal government ordered General Oliver Howard to remove all the Nez Perces to the Lapwai area, which had been set aside in the 1863 Treaty as their reservation.[64]

Toward this end, Lapwai Indian Reservation Agent Monteith sent an embassy from Lapwai, consisting of Head Chief Reuben, who was Chief Joseph's brother-in-law; Chief Ruben's son James Reuben; Whisk-tasket, Chief Joseph's father-in-law; and Captain John, a Nez Perce scout, from Lapwai—to Wallowa to so inform Chief Joseph.[65] These reservation Indians tried to persuade Chief Joseph that reservation life had many advantages and that he should select his land before the best was taken by other non-treaty Indians. After debating overnight, Chief Joseph gave his response:

> I have been talking to the Whites many years about the land in question, and it is strange they cannot understand me. The country they claim belonged to my father, and when he died it was given to me and my people, and I will not leave it until I am compelled to.[66]

Indian Agent Monteith believed that Chief Joseph could not raise over sixty to sixty-five fighting men and, therefore, there would be minimal problems removing the Nez Perce to the reservation. Monteith, in spite of this optimism, believed strong measures were necessary to truly persuade the Nez Perce to give in. He firmly believed that nothing but force would get the Indians to cultivate the soil.

After General Howard delivered his mandate at the council that the Nez Perce had thirty days to gather up their scattered stock and people and report to the reservation, Chief Joseph and his followers returned to the main encampment. They found the Indians greatly agitated because a troop of soldiers was camped nearby. Their uneasiness ignited some of the young warriors to fever pitch. These young men met and talked secretly. Angrily they told one another, "General Howard has shown us the rifle. We answer, 'Yes.' We will stir up a fight for him. We will start his war!"[67]

Other bands joined with Chief Joseph's, and those chiefs supported the young warriors, urging them to fight for their land rather than be driven from it like dogs. Chief Joseph and the Wallowa band elders knew the futility of winning anything by means of war and, speaking against bloodshed, urged the band to move immediately. The young braves and the visiting older chiefs continued to plead for revenge. In the end, Joseph's and the elders' reasoning won out and the word was carried among the lodges by the crier to get ready to move.[68]

Before fleeing to Canada, Chief Joseph's problem was compounded when his followers reminded him he had promised his father he would never sell the land. Chief Joseph had a clear conscience on this point, because he had no intention of selling any land, but if he should be ejected forcibly, he would be breaking no promise in securing the best possible terms for his people.[69] He was a dedicated man; he had sworn to preserve the Wallowa country for his father's people, and he would ultimately face fearful odds in his attempt to do so.

4

INFLUENCE WITH SUPERIORS

Maintains cordial relationships with superiors; has influence with them

---

Joseph's surrender speech, when it reached the papers, touched the country's heart. [70]

The Indian Superintendent, T. B. Odeneal of Oregon, and John B. Monteith, Indian Agent of Lapwai, met with Chief Joseph and his people on March 27, 1873, four years before the Nez Perce flight. The point in question was whether the Nez Perce still owned the Wallowa, and "Joseph's intense sincerity and force of logic soon convinced the government men that something had definitely gone awry in 1863."[71]

They learned that at one period in the history of the Nez Perce, the tribe had had no head chief but was divided into bands, each having a chief or head man, and each claimed, occupied, and held the land within certain natural boundaries.

In 1863, when the whites arbitrarily designated Lawyer as the tribe's head chief because he had signed the treaty, they insisted he had signed away the Wallowa Valley. But did he have that right? Old Chief Joseph said no, and because of the possibility that the Indians might have been right, the government men gave up trying to persuade Old Chief Joseph to move onto the Nez Perce or Umatilla reservation and began discussing the possibility of allowing Chief Joseph and his band to remain in the Wallowa.[72]

In the spring of 1875, General Oliver Howard and Young Chief Joseph met for the first time, neither knowing that in two short years, they would be pitted against each other in the hardest-fought campaign known to Indian warfare. Of this meeting, Howard said:

> Joseph put his large black eyes on my face, and maintained a fixed look for some time. It did not appear to me as an audacious stare; but I thought he was trying to open the windows of his heart to me, and at the same time endeavoring to read my disposition and character. . . . I think Joseph and I became then quite good friends.[73]

In July 1876, when Chief Joseph met Major Henry C. Wood and Lieutenant W. R. Parnell at the Lapwai Reservation, Chief Joseph made a strong and favorable impression on Wood. Both men found it easy to talk to Chief Joseph. He "used the reasoned words of a patriot, made no threats, and bore little resemblance to the sullen, resentful Indians with whom they had clashed on the Plains and in the Southwest. He knew his rights, yet spoke with restraint and dignity."[74]

Major Wood, whose views had been documented and were well known, wrote that the non-treaty Nez Perce "could not in law be bound by the 1863 Treaty, and as far as its attempts to deprive them of the right to the occupancy of any land, those provisions were null and void."[75] He also wrote that the Nez Perce without doubt had the right to reject the treaty of 1855 because the government had violated its obligations under the treaty.

General Howard, well acquainted with this problem, agreed with Major Wood in favor of the Nez Perce claim to the Wallowa. In his report, Howard made it clear that the rescinding of the presidential order of 1873 had been unfair to the Nez Perce.[76]

Chief Joseph, who had been baptized "Ephraim" by Henry Spaulding, was not the menacing savage the government officials expected. During the November 13, 1876, meeting of the government commissioners and Chief Joseph at Lapwai, the commissioners could not help being moved by Chief Joseph. The serious feeling and manner in which he uttered his sentiments impressed them. They also noted that he was "usually calm and sedate, when animated marked and magnetic" and that "an alertness and dexterity in intellectual fencing was exhibited by him that was quite remarkable."[77]

During their flight, following their victory over the Army at Fort Fizzle, the Nez Perce, eager to calm the jittery settlers, were on their best behavior as they rode up the Bitter Root Valley. In Stevensville, they bought supplies, and although the merchants charged exorbitant prices, they paid without protest, spending the profits they had earned as stockmen. Chief Joseph gave up his powder horn just to get a bit of milk to give to the children.[78] Several warriors, entering a ranch house that had been deserted as the bands approached, took two hundred pounds of flour and thirty pounds of coffee. But on orders from their chiefs, they left behind ample payment—seven of their horses. They even used the rancher's branding iron on the animals to make the transaction official. Neither they nor the settlers bothered each other. When some Stevensville citizens later criticized the merchants for selling the supplies, they retorted that the Nez Perce could easily have taken what they wanted without paying for it. And business was business.[79]

When the Nez Perce became lost in Yellowstone Park following the battle of Camas Meadows, they took prisoner a miner named John Shively. Shively ultimately led the Nez Perce back to the proper trail. He later described his adventures. Regarding leadership, he said that "Joseph would come in if it was not for the influences of the others." He described Joseph as "about thirty-five years of age, six feet high, and always in a pleasant mood. . . . Joseph wears one eagle feather."[80]

On the evening of October 4, 1877, before the surrender, Chief Joseph and White Bird reached an understanding. Each would act as he saw fit, with respect to himself and on behalf of his tribesmen. White Bird's disillusionment concerning white men was deep-seated and of long standing. Because the war had been started by members of his band, White Bird feared he would be executed if he surrendered. He did not blame Chief Joseph, however, for attempting to make peace. He said at the decision-making council, "What Joseph does is all right. I have nothing to say."[81]

In a San Francisco *Chronicle* dispatch dated October 10, 1877, Thomas Sutherland reported that, with the assistance of an interpreter, he and Chief Joseph held a long conversation:

> Speaking with Joseph about the Clearwater fight he said that at this place he had fully three hundred men and expected to win the day. He says he wanted to surrender at Kamiah, but he was over powered in the council by others, especially Looking Glass, who painted the picture of the future in such rose colors that he could not resist. . . . I asked him if he bore any ill will toward James Reuben, a Nez Perce Indian who acted as a scout for [the Army] near Kamia, and he answered promptly: "No, a war is a thing where there are two sides. . . ." He says that he himself committed no murders, but on the contrary tried to stop them. . . . He is a temperate man and says that captured whiskey was usually at the bottom of all murders, the Indians getting almost crazy with it and utterly beyond his influence. He was glad to see General Howard, and he felt he would receive justice.[82]

Chester A. Fee wrote of Chief Joseph's generalship that "as a guerilla leader Joseph stands as high as any known in history: [he] ranks with Lee, Jackson, and Grant as one of the best generals this country has produced."[83]

Following the battle at the Bear Paw Mountains, Chief Joseph

> became the monumental symbol of the Nez Perces. They were terrible days for the defeated; full of dejection and suffering, and through the despair and hardship Joseph rose to greatness, never ceasing his efforts to win fair and just treatment for his people.[84]

After the surrender at the Bear Paw:

> Viewing the Indians, still unbowed and proud in the belief that the soldiers had not defeated them, [General] Miles gained a respect for the Nez Perces that he would never lose. "The fight was the most fierce of any Indian engagement I have ever been in," he wrote his wife. " . . . The whole

> Nez Perce movement is unequalled in the history of Indian warfare."[85]

Ex-Sergeant Martin L. Brown related his meeting with Chief Joseph:

> I never met Joseph personally until after the war was over. I was on a detail that took nineteen Indian prisoners to Fort Lapwai, Idaho. . . . When we delivered the prisoners to Joseph, he shook hands with each one of our detail, and appeared quite friendly. He apparently felt no resentment toward the soldiers. His manner was grave, and he had the air of one used to being respected. All the Indians in the camp showed deference toward him and seemed to like him. Joseph was an honest man, and really believed the government unjustly took his land from him. As for the war, he thought he was doing right by fighting for his ancestral lands and finally for his liberty.[86]

In the spring of 1904, Chief Joseph attended the commencement exercises at Carlisle Indian Industrial School in Pennsylvania and sat at a banquet table with General Howard. Chief Joseph, speaking at the dinner, said:

> Friends, I meet here my friend, General Howard. I used to be so anxious to meet him. I wanted to kill him in war. Today I am glad to meet him . . . and to be friends with General Howard. We are both old men, still we live and I am glad. We both fought in many wars and we are both alive. Ever since the war I have made up my mind to be friendly to the whites and to everybody. I wish you, my friends, would believe me as I believe myself in my heart in what I say. When my friend, General Howard, and I fought together, I had no idea that we would ever sit down to a meal together, as today, but we have, and I am glad. I have lost many friends, and many men, women and children, but I have no grievance against any of the white people,

> General Howard, or any one [*sic*]. If General Howard dies first, of course I will be sorry.[87]

On June 12, 1956, the Chief Joseph Dam on the Columbia River below Bridgeport, Washington, was officially named and dedicated. Erskine Wood, who as a boy spent two summers with Chief Joseph, said of him: "His chieftainship was never in question. As he had all through his life, he led his people by his wisdom and the quiet force and dignity of his character."[88]

5

INITIATION OF STRUCTURE

Clearly defines own role, and lets followers know what is expected

The long trail of tears had begun for Joseph and his tribespeople.[89]

At the November 1876 council at Lapwai, Idaho, before the Nez Perce flight to Canada, Chief Joseph told General Howard:

> Do not misunderstand me, but understand me fully with reference to my affection for the land. I never said the land was mine to do with as I chose. The one who has a right to dispose of it is the one who created it. I claim a right to live on my land, and accord you the privilege to live on yours.[90]

Chief Joseph tried to explain to General Howard thirty days was insufficient time for the Nez Perce to find and move their scattered stock, and to gather supplies for the coming winter.

Chief Joseph's Own Story reveals Howard's response: "If you are not here in that time, I shall consider that you want to fight, and will send my soldiers to drive you on."

Chief Joseph replied: "War can be avoided and it ought to be avoided. I want no war. My people have always been the friends of the white man. Why are you in such a hurry? Let us wait until fall, then the river will be low."

General Howard answered: "If you let the time run over one day, the soldiers will be there to drive you onto the reservation."[91]

Unfortunately, when Howard issued his thirty-day ultimatum, it was springtime; rivers were high. Ignoring Chief Joseph's plea that they be allowed to wait until the waters lowered, Howard ordered them out. With such limited time allotted them, the Nez Perce abandoned many horses and cattle in the Wallowa Valley. As they crossed the swollen Snake River, they had to force thousands of cattle and horses into the fast-flowing stream, and dozens more animals drowned.

In the valley, the settlers were overjoyed. The Indians were going. The Wallowa at last was to be the domain of the white man. Some of the stockmen rode cautiously after the Indians, stopping on high land to spy on their withdrawal. Occasionally, they came on Indian stock, overlooked by the Nez Perce. No one knows how many head of horses and cattle were appropriated by the settlers, driven back to the rangeland in the valley or rounded up in the canyons after the Indians had departed.[92]

Nez Perce resentment increased.

During the enforced march, Chief Joseph's band stopped at White Bird's camp in Rocky Canyon by the Salmon River—the "River of No Return"[93]—where other non-treaty bands had also gathered. At nearby Lake Tepahlewan, the Nez Perce settled in for a ten-day council. During these discussions, Chief Joseph never wavered in arguing for peace. He knew only too well that the Army's strength far outweighed that of the Nez Perce.

While thus encamped, young Nez Perce warriors spoke bitter words against the whites. They demanded war to avenge their wrongs. Chief Joseph, insisting upon peace, was accused of cowardice by some of the men. Chief Joseph, however, had other things on his mind. One of his two wives was about to give birth; he also had to butcher a beef so his family could eat.

While Chief Joseph was off from the council attending to these matters, some of the young men, becoming drunk from whiskey they had bought from white settlers, began to conduct a parade ceremony. Riding around the camp, they showed off their battle trophies and proudly recounted their war deeds. Walatitis, whose father had been killed by A. B. Findley and Wells McNall after accusing him of stealing their horses, was riding in the parade. An old man began to taunt him, telling him that if he were so brave, he should avenge his father's death rather than stage mock war parades.[94]

The young Indian, accompanied by his friends Isapsis-ilpilp and Um-til-ilp-cown, all members of White Bird's band, accepted the challenge and rode off to Slate Creek. There they killed Richard Devine, a retired sailor who had taken over Indian lands in a narrow canyon and liked to command his half-wild dogs to attack any Indian who traveled past his place. The next day they killed three more settlers and wounded another. On June 14, they returned to camp with the victims' guns and horses. Seeing their success, Too-hool-hool-suit and seventeen more warriors joined the original three and killed or wounded several more settlers. Some of the Indians, wishing to avoid war, left the camp and went to Lapwai. They advised Chief Joseph to do the same, but he said he couldn't, that the white people would blame him.

> "I was deeply grieved," he recalled later. "I knew that their acts would involve all my people. I saw that the war could not be prevented. I counseled peace from the beginning. I knew that we were too weak to fight the United States. We had many grievances, but I knew that war would bring more. . . . We hoped the white settlers would not join the soldiers. Before the war commenced, we had discussed this matter, and many of my people were in favor of warning them that if they took no part against us, they should not be molested in the event of war being begun by General Howard. This plan was voted down in the war counsel. I would have given my own life if I could have undone the killing of white men by my people."[95]

Chief Joseph thus acknowledged the warriors' guilt but pointed out that Howard was also to blame. Had he not forced them from the valley with his thirty-day ultimatum, which did not allow them time to gather their scattered stock, there would have been no war. "It may never again be our home," he said, "but my father sleeps there, and I love it as I love my mother. I left there, hoping to avoid bloodshed."[96]

The Nez Perce leaders realized that General Howard would retaliate for these killings. Rather than wait to be attacked by his military forces, they decided to escape across the Rockies, perhaps to Canada, where Sitting Bull was living in exile.[97] Before they could finish their preparations for departure, the soldiers attacked them.

This fight came about because news of the murders of the four whites was relayed to the towns of Mount Idaho, Cottonwood, and Fort Lapwai. Under orders from Howard, Colonel David Perry left Fort Lapwai with ninety soldiers, heading for White Bird Canyon. At the same time, Howard sent a messenger 120 miles to telegraph a call for reinforcements from Walla Walla and Fort Vancouver. Howard telegraphed General McDowell in San Francisco, detailing what had happened and ending, "Think we will make short work of it."[98] Regarding this confidence, Gulick, in *Chief Joseph Country*, comments, "Custer had thought that, too."[99]

Knowing the attack was coming, Chief Joseph gathered the Nez Perce at a spot where the Salmon River and White Bird Creek joined. Colonel David Perry, commander of Fort Lapwai, was in charge of the raid. When the soldiers arrived, Perry saw nothing suspicious and started his troops toward the camp, unaware the Indians were prepared for his arrival.

White Bird and his braves had concealed themselves in a ravine to the left of a spot beyond which the soldiers would have to pass. Ollicut, Chief Joseph's younger brother—"the leader of the young men"[100]—and his group were positioned to the right. Most of the soldiers were walking, leading their horses, even though they were "mounted troops." As the troopers approached the camp, one struck a match to light his pipe. The waiting Indian guards saw the flame and gave a coyote howl. The battle was precipitated when six warriors approached the soldiers under a flag of truce and one of the volunteer civilians, "a man wearing a broad, whitish hat and riding a white horse"[101] fired a shot. The Indians fired in return. Many of these soldiers had never seen combat, and they fled in panic for a complete rout. The Indians followed them twenty miles, all the way to the outskirts of Mount Idaho. Thirty-three soldiers and one officer were killed and seven wounded. The Indians suffered light, if any, casualties. Wohlrabe says, "At White Bird Canyon, the Indians won a decisive victory over four hundred soldiers under General Oliver Otis Howard's command."[102]

Only Custer's ill-fated battle in 1876 had ended with such disastrous results to the white Army. This battle proved to the troops that the Nez Perce were not cowards and were far more disciplined than the Army. When it came to obeying orders and carrying out a battle plan, their war chief had proven himself a master tactician. This one defeat convinced Howard that, man for man, the Nez Perce were at least the equal of his best troops. What they lacked in drill and discipline, they more than made up by their accuracy of aim, an unusual trait in mounted Indians.[103]

One of the Army officers reported:

> Joseph's party was thoroughly disciplined; that they rode at full gallop along the mountain side in a steady formation by fours; formed twos, at a given signal, with perfect precision, to cross a narrow bridge; galloped into line, reined in to a sudden halt, and dismounted with as much system as regulars.[104]

Chief Joseph had won his first battle.

Following Perry's defeat at White Bird Creek, Howard began rounding up reinforcements. An artillery detachment coming home from Alaska was rerouted; troops from San Francisco were summoned. Within a short time, he had gathered an additional two hundred men, including troops of volunteers from every place he could secure them within a two-hundred-mile radius. Before the war was over, troops would be called from five additional Pacific Northwest forts and from Arizona. The Second Infantry would be called from Atlanta, Georgia.[105] He also had two hundred regular cavalry, infantry, and volunteers, as well as two Gatling guns. All he lacked was Chief Joseph. The Indians were gone, leaving behind clear signs they had crossed the turbulent Salmon River and now were on the loose in the wild, rugged country to the south and west.[106]

Chief Joseph was actually traveling to the ancient homeland of the Nez Perce, the Middle Fork of the Clearwater River. Howard found them at a point east of the Clearwater River and southeast of Kamiah.

Here Chief Joseph had carefully selected a spot for the next battle. To the front was a vast open space the troops would have to pass over to reach the Indians. Behind and to the sides were wooded canyons to which the Nez Perce could pull back, if necessary. They had also dug rifle pits and erected log barricades.

Chiefs White Bird, Looking Glass, and Black Eagle, impressed by Chief Joseph's victory over Perry, had joined their bands to Chief Joseph's. These additions increased the number of warriors to three hundred, all of whom were armed with modern breech-loading rifles, and all of whom were waiting for the soldiers. At noon on July 11, Howard and four hundred men attacked.

The response of the Nez Perce, firing from hillsides and ravines, was described by Howard's adjutant, Lieutenant Henry Clay Wood:

> Their brown naked bodies were seen flying from shelter to shelter. Their yells were incessant as they cheered each other on or signalled a successful shot.[107]

Such tactics as rock entrenchments, and the besieging of superior numbers of troops, were never known before in Indian warfare. The battle continued until dark and picked up with fierce fighting the next day. When the toll reached four Indians killed and six injured, and thirty-seven troopers wounded or killed, the Indians pulled back to the canyons. Lieutenant William R. Parnell wrote:

> At the "Clearwater" the opposing forces were about equal. If anything the troops had the advantage in numbers as well as position. And yet, strictly speaking, the Indians were not defeated. Their loss must have been insignificant and their retreat to Kamai was masterly, deliberate, and unmolested, leaving us with victory barren of results.[108]

On July 12, Howard realized that only a token force opposed him, so he ordered his troops to advance. The Nez Perce warriors gave ground steadily but made certain that the women and children had time to get away north toward Kamiah. When the soldiers reached the deserted campsite, they found a few teepees, utensils, food supplies, and clothing. Thomas Sutherland, the newspaper reporter accompanying Howard, sent back a story describing these articles and added: "For my part I found a much worn pair of small moccasins and an absurd little rag doll under a tree."[109]

The next day, Howard followed close behind during the Indian retreat toward Kamiah. He put Captain Charles Rawn, commander of Fort Missoula, in charge of the attack. Rawn barricaded the Lolo Trail but was unable to follow through because the Nez Perce displayed a truce flag, asking the terms of surrender. Through Rawn, Howard informed them it was to be unconditional surrender, nothing less. The Nez Perce warriors replied that they intended no harm; they only wished to pass unimpeded to the buffalo country where they could find new homes. The volunteers riding with Rawn had no objections whatsoever to granting the proposal. Rawn, however, could not disobey the orders given him. The warriors discussed the situation with Rawn for two more days. On the third day, Rawn prepared his troops to attack.

W. R. Logan was an eyewitness to the results:

> About ten o'clock we heard singing, apparently above our heads. Upon looking up we discovered the Indians passing along the side of the cliff, where we thought a goat could not pass, much less an entire tribe of Indians with all their impediments. The entire band dropped into the valley beyond us and then proceeded up the Bitter Root. Two civilians and I rode down from our camp and followed with the Indians for a mile or more. They were good-natured, cracked jokes, and seemed very much amused at the way they had fooled Rawn and Logan.[110]

While the three-day talks were going on, Chief Joseph had scouted the area and discovered how to bypass the soldiers. He had his band zigzag along a series of gulches to the right of the barricade, while the other warriors were parleying with the troops. Rawn's fortification later became known as Fort Fizzle.[111]

In one of his reports, General William T. Sherman describes the campaign as "one of the most extraordinary Indian wars of which there is any record. The Indians throughout displayed a courage and skill that elicited universal praise."[112]

After crossing the Lolo Trail, the Nez Perce debated which way to go—to the buffalo country, to the Old Woman Country (Canada), or through the Bitter Root Valley. When asked for his choice, Chief Joseph said, "Since we have left our own country, it matters little where we go." In his mind, they were now a people in exile.[113]

On July 17, Chief Joseph continued the trek toward the traditional buffalo hunting grounds of the Nez Perce. His route took his people over two major mountain ranges and caused endless problems for Howard. The Army trailed far behind Chief Joseph. The terrain made hauling supplies by pack train a necessity. Howard took ten days to gather sufficient supplies and animals, and as he started into the mountains, the Nez Perce left the pass on the other side.

The next route of the Nez Perce took them to the Valley of the Big Horn River on the Montana side of the Bitter Root Mountains. Here, the telegraph again proved an enemy to the fleeing Indians. Howard signaled General John Gibbon in Missoula; Gibbon and two hundred soldiers began following Chief Joseph's trail.

At dawn on August 9, Gibbon attacked the Nez Perce encampment at the Big Hole. The soldiers began clubbing and shooting all Indians within reach, including women and children. Walatitis and Isapsis-ilp-ilp, the members of White Bird's band who initiated the Slate Creek attacks directly leading to the Nez Perce flight, were killed in this battle.

Chief Joseph and his people fled to the willow thickets, leaving Gibbon and his men to take over their camp. The troopers attempted to burn the lodges, but especially heavy dew prevented the structures from catching fire. The soldiers then dragged all the Indians' possessions out of the lodges and set fire to these belongings.

Chief Joseph, however, wasn't finished. He positioned his warriors to fire into the troops from three sides, driving them from the village and eventually surrounding them in the timber. The Nez Perce women and children, in spite of the heavy fire of the soldiers, re-entered the camp to collect their remaining possessions before retreating down the valley. Gibbon pulled his men back, sustaining serious injury in the process. The following morning, Howard's reinforcements arrived, ending the battle.

Records indicate Gibbon lost thirty-one soldiers and had thirty-eight wounded; Chief Joseph lost nineteen warriors and seventy women and children on the battlefield. Gibbon, briefing Howard on the Big Hole battle, concluded:

> And here you find us, some killed, many wounded, but in no way discouraged. It was a gallant struggle. Who would have believed those Indians would have rallied after such a surprise and made such a fight?[114]

While Howard cooled his heels, waiting for additional reinforcements, the Nez Perce headed across the Bitter Root Mountains into Idaho, reaching Camas Meadows, near the western entrance to Yellowstone National Park. Accounts differ whether Chief Joseph participated in the Camas Meadows fight that followed, but when it was over, an unidentified soldier wrote, "It must be admitted that Joseph worsted us."[115] On August 18, Howard learned that the Nez Perce were camped eighteen miles east of the Army's encampment at Dry Creek Station. Reaching Camas Meadows on the 19th, Howard, confident of victory, posted night pickets completely around the camp to cut off the Nez Perce retreat and staked the horses and mules out to graze.

Afterward, General Howard gave his account of the raid that followed:

> Joseph had so organized a few of his Indians, and marched them toward camp, as to make the picket think it was Bacon's party coming back. They, the Indians, came on by fours, steadily, and very like our troopers, till challenged. Not being able to reply correctly, the picket fired upon them. This was doubtless the first sound. Then came the

> big firing and yelling, and then, quickly enough, the reply from our camp.[116]

Gulick says:

> Never mind that the Nez Perce knew nothing about Lieutenant Bacon's party, that Joseph was not even in the raiding group, and that it was Otskai who fired the premature shot. General Howard's story made a very clever fellow out of that red rascal Joseph, but not quite clever enough to learn the secret password and fool an alert picket.[117]

The morning following the raid, General Howard ordered three companies of cavalry to pursue the Indians, bring them to bay, do battle with them, and recover the stolen mules. Since twenty of the mules proved too contrary to drive, the Indians, who disliked mules anyway, left them behind for the soldiers to recapture. Five miles from the soldiers' camp, a dozen Nez Perce warriors lay in ambush. Two of the companies spread right and left in an attempt to flank the Indians. But Nez Perce reinforcements arrived and *they* spread right and left, outflanking the flankers and pouring a withering fire into the soldiers. Having finally finished breakfast, General Howard and the rest of his command rode forward to see how the battle was going. When Howard learned that Major Sanford had withdrawn and left Captain Norwood's company surrounded by an overwhelming force of hostile Indians, he ordered a charge by the entire command. With Norwood's company rescued and the Nez Perce withdrawing, Howard led his troops back to Camas Meadows. During the fight, the Nez Perce had not lost a man. The military lost three men killed, five wounded, and one hundred eighty pack mules stolen.[118]

General Howard's troops were in no condition to go on with the pursuit until he had replenished his supplies and re-outfitted his soldiers. The men were exhausted from the long chase, their boots worn out, their clothing ragged and not warm enough for the high mountain country they were in. Howard's only consolation was that

Captain Bacon and his forty men were waiting for the Nez Perce in Targhee Pass—or so he thought.

The Nez Perce were deeply disappointed that they had stolen mules instead of horses. However, their brilliantly concocted and boldly undertaken scheme had so badly damaged Howard's command that those particular troops would never again get close enough to the escaping bands to see their dust, let alone engage them in battle. Gulick says, "Which probably was just as well."[119]

Alvin Josephy says that Howard's pursuit of the Nez Perce had now become a national drama. To some it was a joke. Others expressed admiration for the Nez Perce, delighting in the David–Goliath similarities and mocking the tribulations and bungling of the Army:

> Time and again the Indians, burdened with baggage, women, children, and a large horse herd, had outrun and outwitted the best that the army could put against them, and the easy way in which a small number of Indian warriors had doubled back and stolen Howard's mules from under his nose had seemed to . . . be comic opera at its best.[120]

Colonel Samuel D. Sturgis of the Seventh Cavalry now joined the chase. "During the night [at Hart Mountain], Joseph sent a few of his young men around Sturgis' force. . . . At daybreak they stirred up a great dust by tying sagebrush to their lariats and riding furiously, dragging the bundles of brush along the ground."[121] Sturgis, convinced he was on the heels of the main band, headed south after them. This trick left the mouth of the pass to the north open and the Nez Perce filed through. The brush draggers rejoined Chief Joseph at a point between the Yellowstone and Missouri Rivers. They then crossed the Yellowstone toward the Musselshell Basin.

Meanwhile, Chief Joseph forged ahead and entered Yellowstone Park. There, the Nez Perce, unfamiliar with the area, became lost. Chief Joseph captured a miner named Shivley and pressed him into service to lead the Indians back toward their path to the buffalo hunting grounds, promising that he would be released unharmed. He was treated well and said Joseph was very pleasant to him, always meeting him with a nod and a smile. He later provided details of his adventure with the Nez Perce:

> They had bread, no meat, scouse, camas and tea of shrubs. They were going to the Crow country but did not know the route. . . . Every lodge drives its own horses in front of it when traveling, each lodge keeping its own bands separate. . . . About one-sixth of the horses have sore backs or are disabled. . . . They keep no scouts ahead.[122]

On August 26, 1877, General William T. Sherman telegraphed to General Philip H. Sheridan in Chicago: "I don't think Howard's troops will catch Joseph, but they will follow, trusting to your troops heading them off when they come out on the east of the mountains."[123]

At Canyon Creek, the Army attacked the Nez Perce once more. Forced to retreat, the warriors delayed the troops long enough to allow the women, children, and old men to escape. A 150-mile running battle ensued before the Nez Perce once more shook off the Army.

At the close of the Canyon Creek fighting on September 13, the soldiers returned to the field hospital at the mouth of Canyon Creek. They found that the Crows, with whom the Nez Perce hoped to join, had "borrowed" many of the soldiers' personal belongings and several horses and pack animals. "The Crows took no part in the fight," Stanton G. Fisher, a civilian scout, complained, "but staid in the rear and stole every thing [*sic*] they could get their hands on."[124] At this point Howard, Sturgis, Colonel Gilbert, and General Nelson Miles and their respective troops were all pursuing Chief Joseph's band. Howard now employed some strategy of his own. He slowed his pace, having observed that when he slowed, the Nez Perce slowed; when he increased speed, the Nez Perce did likewise. When Howard's soldiers came upon the Nez Perce scouts, the troopers fled in an all-out rout, leaving their horses behind to trick the Nez Perce into thinking that the rest of the Army was far behind and had given up the chase.

Accordingly, Chief Joseph slowed, unaware that Miles, with a Napoleon cannon and breech-loading Hotchkiss gun, was traveling rapidly to intercept him. Miles' force, despite their unsuccessful pursuit of the Nez Perce for several weeks, was highly optimistic that this time they would capture "Joseph's Nez Perces."[125]

Two civilian guides described General Miles' appearance:

> He looked the leader he was—rough, tough and ready. Weighing nearly 200 pounds, he sat his charger like a centaur, his brown mustache and side whiskers, slightly mixed with gray, adorned features that are heavy but pleasing . . . overshadowed by a broad-brimmed slouched drab hat. A wide blue ribbon encircled its crown, with blue streamers behind. He wore a red blanket frontier shirt and a black necktie, its ends floating over his shoulders; outside the shirt, a buckskin coat, short at the hips and carelessly buttoned; the light blue trousers of a private soldier, with black stripes down the seams, and coarse boots completed his attire.[126]

On September 23, the band crossed the Missouri River and camped in the Bear Paw Mountains on Snake Creek, approximately forty miles from the Canadian border. Miles, meanwhile, kept the Little Rockies Range between the Indians and himself and ordered Cheyenne scouts up the ridges to spy on Chief Joseph's movements. On September 30, at 8:00 a.m., Miles's troops attacked the camp of nearly seven hundred people. Of these individuals, approximately two hundred fifty were warriors. All the others were women, children, and the old. Secure in their belief that Howard's army was too far away to attack them, some of the men were off hunting while the women prepared the buffalo meat from a hunt the day before. Joseph and his twelve-year-old daughter, Kapkap Ponmi (Noise of Running Feet),[127] were rounding up horses while others packed for the trip north. Children played with sticks and mud balls while some of the villagers finished breakfast. Two scouts sounded the alarm when they discovered the approaching soldiers. "Soon, from the south came a noise," recalled Yellow Wolf, "a rumble like stampeding buffaloes."[128]

The warriors had learned to dig trenches after the Big Hole fight and had here constructed a series of underground shelters connected by galleries. These galleries "explain why the Indians' casualties were not greater, and why they were able to hold off the superior force of soldiers for five days."[129]

"We digged the trenches with camas hooks and butcher knives," an unnamed woman survivor explained. "With pans we threw out the dirt."[130]

In 1879, Chief Joseph said of this battle:

> We had no knowledge of Miles' army until a short time before he made a charge upon us, cutting our camp in two and capturing nearly all of our horses. . . . About seventy men, myself among them, were cut off. My little daughter, twelve years of age, was with me. I gave her a rope, and told her to catch a horse and join the others who were cut off from camp. I have not seen her since, but I have learned she is alive and well. I thought of my wife and children, who were now surrounded by soldiers, and I resolved to go to them or die. With a prayer in my mouth to the Great Spirit Chief who rules above, I dashed unharmed through the line of soldiers. It seemed to me that there were guns on every side, before and behind me. My clothes were cut to pieces and my horse was wounded, but I was not hurt. As I reached the door of my lodge, my wife handed me my rifle, saying, "Here's your gun. Fight!"[131]

Even though he had become separated from his family and had no idea what was happening to them, Joseph collected his men and encouraged them to fight for the women and children. The Nez Perce retreated to their galleries, holding their fire until the soldiers were within one hundred yards before they blasted their first volley at the oncoming troopers. The soldiers promptly retreated. The Nez Perce warriors specifically aimed at Army officers. Having learned in previous battles that they were the ones giving spoken commands, these soldiers were their first targets. Following the first charge, only one officer remained unhurt. Accounts of the total Nez Perce dead vary, but records concur that twenty-two men, women, and children died during the first twenty-four hours of the battle. In all, the Army suffered fifty-three officers and enlisted men dead or wounded.[132]

The situation now became desperate for the Nez Perce. With the Army in possession of their camp, they had no shelter from the Arctic winds.

When Howard arrived at Miles's camp on the evening of October 4, snow was falling heavily. He learned that Miles had begun surrender negotiations with Chief Joseph, and told him to keep on, that he (Howard) would not take over the command until Chief Joseph surrendered; Miles would receive full credit for the capture.[133]

Major Henry Clay Wood, General Howard's adjutant, recorded that at mid-afternoon on October 5, 1877, Chief Joseph, with a guard of five warriors, rode up to General Miles:

> His scalp-lock was tied with otter fur, and the rest of his hair hung in thick braids on each side of his head. He wore buckskin leggings and a gray woolen shawl, containing four or five bullet holes. His head and wrist also showed scratches from bullets. . . . The soldiers observed that the chief's clothes were pierced by more than a dozen bullet holes.[134]

His hands were crossed on the pommel of his saddle, and his Winchester carbine lay across his knees. He approached with bowed head, but as he reached Howard and Miles, he straightened and gracefully dismounted. When he offered his rifle to Howard, Howard motioned that he should give it to Miles. Then "those present shook hands with Joseph, whose worn and anxious face lighted with a sad smile as silently he took each offered hand. Presently turning away, he walked to the tent provided for him."[135]

Following Chief Joseph's surrender of his rifle to Miles, Howard asked the friendly Sioux to run down all of the groups of Nez Perce that were hiding in the hills, but the Sioux refused. A few of the fugitives were later captured, but at least one hundred managed to escape.[136]

Chief Joseph was "in great distress" over the whereabouts of his daughter, who had escaped during the initial attack. She was wearing very little clothing at the time, and he was afraid she would freeze to death.[137] She actually made it to Canada with a group of other Nez Perce.[138] In the late spring of 1878, some of the Nez Perce who had escaped to Canada at the time of the surrender returned to the United States. Chief Joseph's daughter Kapkap Ponmi was one of these returnees.[139]

No one can pinpoint with certainty the number of Indians who surrendered with Joseph. The difficulty lies in separating children from adults, and losses through death. Army records indicate 87 warriors—40 of them wounded—184 women, and 147 children arrived at Fort Leavenworth, Kansas, to begin their internment.[140] Chief White Bird and several others had fled to Canada. Looking Glass and Chief Joseph's younger brother, Ollicut, had died fighting. The band had been one day's hard travel from the Canadian border. Perhaps it was to the telegraph that Chief Joseph owed his final defeat, for all of his skill and courage in defeating human enemies could not outwit this foe.

Official casualty lists showed that 127 soldiers and approximately 50 civilians were killed, and 147 soldiers were wounded. Chief Joseph's total losses have been estimated at 151 killed and 88 wounded. The exact number of Nez Perce has never been precisely tallied because of the women and children dead and wounded; those numbers were unknown. The Nez Perce surrendered eleven hundred horses, one hundred saddles, more than one hundred guns, and various other articles. Francis Haines asks, "Was half the Wallowa worth the price?"[141]

General Miles remained a staunch friend to Chief Joseph. He was constantly recommending that the band be sent back to Idaho, or even to the Wallowa. Public interest grew after the publication of "Chief Joseph's Own Story" in 1879. At length public sentiment reached such a pitch that some of the widows and orphans were permitted to return to Lapwai in the summer of 1882.[142]

The Nez Perce surrender at the Bear Paw Mountains provided the victorious government officials with a vexing problem. They realized, belatedly, that their prisoners must be fed, sheltered, and provided with a place to live. Initially, they were transferred overland to Fort Keogh in eastern Montana. But General Philip Sheridan decided that maintaining them there would be too expensive, so in November 1877, he commanded they be sent first to Fort Buford, then to Fort Lincoln, near Bismark, North Dakota.

On the train taking them to Fort Lincoln, the cars were crowded and the train had to stop frequently so that the Indians could drink at the water tanks. At one such stop, the train pulled away without anyone realizing Chief Joseph was not yet back on board. When they discovered he was missing, the train stopped, backed up, and came upon Chief Joseph running down the tracks after it. He had chosen to remain with his people rather than escape.[143]

After a stay in Bismark, the Nez Perce were next sent to Fort Leavenworth in eastern Kansas. Chief Joseph, upon learning of the plan, said, "When will these white chiefs tell the truth?"[144]

At Fort Leavenworth, where more than twenty of them died of malaria, the Nez Perce were held as prisoners of war until the spring of 1878. The problem of what to do with them intensified. They could not be held as prisoners of war forever. They could not be sent back to the Wallowa Valley because the white settlers had issued legal charges against them. Indian Territory—which had for decades been the dumping ground for tribes uprooted by relocation or war—became the next solution. They were moved to the Quapaw Reservation in Kansas. The commissioners decided the temperature change between the two locations was negligible. Chief Joseph disagreed. By October, forty-seven more Nez Perce had died. When comparing the humid, malaria-ridden Quapaw Reservation to the healthful, temperate Wallowa Valley, he said, "I think very little of this country. It is like a poor man; it amounts to nothing."[145] In June 1879 they were moved to the Oklahoma Reserve.

Finally, in May 1885, 118 Nez Perce who accepted Christianity were allowed to return to the Lapwai reservation in Idaho, which was now under the control of Charles Monteith, a straight-laced Presbyterian who wanted no rebels on his reservation. Long hair and spirited horses were symbols of dissent, which he would not accept.[146] The 150 non-treaty Nez Perce, including Chief Joseph, who retained their old tribal ways instead of cutting their hair and accepting Christianity, were sent to the Colville reservation in Washington Territory.[147] When the group was divided, according to Yellow Wolf, "the interpreter asked us, 'Where you want to go? Lapwai and be Christian, or Colville and just be yourself?'"[148]

Chief Joseph, a member of the Colville group, frequently traveled from Nespelem, Washington, to visit the Lapwai reservation. The missionaries working with the reservation Indians at Lapwai disliked his visits because his were not the virtues reservation and church officials regarded as most important at that time. Lapwai Indians, and others, greatly esteeming Chief Joseph, wanted to hear his tales of valor and deeds of heroism. "In this regard, Joseph was quite reticent."[149]

In November 1883, the Presbyterian General Assembly decided to send Dr. George Spining to assess the Nez Perce situation on the Quapaw Reservation. Arriving there, Spining went to the children's graveyard with the minister to see for himself the extent of the tragedy the Nez Perce had suffered. The minister pointed to two small mounds of earth. The graves were those of his two young children who had died since coming to Indian Territory. A third child of his was clinging to life at that very moment. Spining counted almost a hundred graves. A single bell tinkled mournfully above one of the small mounds. When Spining glanced up, a solitary figure on horseback was observing him. "Keep this in your heart," the man told him. "Tell it to the Great Father in Washington, that maybe his heart will be touched and he will take pity upon this suffering people."

The solitary figure was Joseph.[150]

6

INTEGRATION

Maintains a closely knit organization, resolves intermember conflicts

He talked but little, but . . . when he spoke to an Indian, there was no hesitancy about obeying him.[151]

After the Lapwai council in May 1877 when the Nez Perce agreed to move to the reservation, Joseph faced the problem of getting his people to accede to the move because the Nez Perce did not recognize the principle of majority rule. A majority decision among the Indians did not automatically deem acceptance of the issue among the individuals. Rather, those who disagreed had the privilege of going elsewhere and doing something different if they wished.

Haines says:

> In all the Nez Perce tribe, no chief had ever had the power to say to his people "Come" or "Go" according to his wish. They were not rulers giving orders, but leaders who must gain consent to their plans by persuasion, by reasonable arguments, by force of personality. . . . If in council the tribe or band are pleased with the council and advice . . . they follow it. If it does not accord with their feelings, it is disregarded. It speaks well for Joseph's personality and his ability as a speaker that on this occasion he was able to

> persuade the entire band to accept his advice after a short discussion.[152]

When the Findley–McNall trial was finally held for the murder of Wil-hau-tyah, Judge Brainard freed Findley, ruling that he had acted in self-defense. The verdict disturbed Findley, who knew that the Indians would not be satisfied. At his own request, he was heard in October by a grand jury at Union but was again exonerated. By the end of October, he was back with his family in the Wallowa, and the case was ended.[153]

Chief Joseph's own words made his feelings clear:

> With reference to . . . the white man who committed the deed . . . I have come to the conclusion to let him escape and enjoy health, and not take his life for the one he took. . . . I do not want anything in payment for the deed he committed. I pronounce the sentence that he should live. I spoke to the murderer and told him I thought a great deal of the land on which he had shed the blood of one of my people. When I saw all the settlers take the murderer's part . . . I told them there was no law in favor of murder. I could see they were all in favor of the murder, so I told them to leave the country. I told them it was of great importance. You see one of our bodies lying dead . . . [and] I cannot leave that country and go elsewhere.[154]

In Yellowstone Park, on August 23, 1877, five warriors, members of a scouting party under the leadership of Chief Joseph's nephew, discovered a group of tourists who were exploring the "wonders of geyserland."[155] After a debate of what to do with the whites, the Indians took them prisoner and placed them "under the personal protection of Chief Joseph."[156] One of the captives who was introduced to Chief Joseph noted: "The chief has a high forehead, a straight prominent nose, high cheekbones, and when he speaks, he sets his lips together with a firmness that showed he meant what he said."[157]

Emma Cowan, one of the captives, later described the August 24 trek of the Nez Perce over Mary Mountain:

> Over this mountain range, almost impassable because of the dense timber, several hundred head of loose horses, pack horses, camp accoutrements, and the five or six hundred Indians were trying to force a passage. . . . It was a feat few white people could have accomplished without axe or implements of some sort to cut the way. It required constant watching to prevent the loose horses from straying away. . . . The pack animals also caused trouble, often getting wedged in between trees. An old woman would pound them on the head until they backed out. And such yelling! Their lungs seemed in excellent condition.[158]

During the peace negotiations on October 5, 1877, the Nez Perce warriors debated whether to keep fighting or to surrender. During their discussions, a messenger from Howard's encampment reported that the Army wanted no more fighting, that Howard had said, "We will have no more war!"[159]

This decree provided the solution to the Indians' problem: They could agree to ending the battle without giving the appearance of a forced surrender. Chief Joseph said, "You see, it is true, I did not say, 'Let's quit!'" as he had been accused.

Yellow Wolf said this line of reasoning convinced most of the warriors. They said, "Yes, we believe you now."[160] It was a significant point to the Indians, for to their understanding Chief Joseph was saying that they would not surrender but would merely agree with Miles and Howard to end the fighting. "It would be a draw and they could go back to their homes with honor."[161]

After the surrender at the Bear Paw Mountains, many of the Nez Perce slipped away from their captors and escaped to Canada. Chief Joseph, likewise, "could have escaped, but he chose to become an honorable prisoner of war and remain with his people as their tribal guardian."[162]

White Bird had talked to Chief Joseph in the morning before the surrender and persuaded Joseph to give himself up first by promising that after he had finished supervising the surrender of the other Indians, he (White Bird) too, would surrender. However, the night of the same day that Chief Joseph surrendered, White Bird instead escaped to Canada by slipping past the soldier guard in the dark. Howard, when he learned of White Bird's escape, insisted that the surrender terms granted all those who had turned themselves in were voided by White Bird's treachery. This was certainly an unfair assumption. Chief Joseph, placed under guard in Howard's camp, could not possibly have directed the actions of any other Indians, most particularly those individuals who belonged to other bands. Chief Joseph pointed out, uselessly, that he was responsible only for his own men. Howard, not Chief Joseph, was responsible for overseeing the prisoners and making terms with White Bird.[163]

Following the death of Looking Glass in the battle of Bear Paw and White Bird's escape to Canada, Chief Joseph "spoke in the first person singular when referring to his role of leadership. This usage did not signify a change in the man, but rather in the circumstances."[164]

After his final refusal to cut his hair and accept Christianity, Chief Joseph settled down to reservation life in Nespelem, Washington. He maintained a large patriarchal household by inviting nephews and others to share his home. The government built a house for him, a "small, rough-board, battened house and a barn on the farm he selected about four miles from the sub-agency."[165] Chief Joseph, however, chose to live in his lodge, as he had done all his life.

Deer hunting was an important tribal activity. Joseph distributed the meat according to need, but the hide became the sole property of the one who had killed the deer. The young were instructed in history, religion, and the arts. Joseph advised the young people to learn both the old and the new ways. He was, Beal says, "considerate and kind toward all, and highly revered. He had no official authority, but his personality enforced his decisions. He presided upon all festival occasions, and he spoke eloquently."[166]

The march had lasted from June 27 to October 5, 1877. General Miles, under higher orders, did not keep his promise to Chief Joseph that in the spring the Nez Perce would be allowed to return to their country with their remaining stock. However, the two remained close friends and respected each other's character and abilities. When President Grant died on July 23, 1885, Miles asked Chief Joseph, who was visiting Washington, DC in an attempt to get back his reservation, to ride by his side at the head of the funeral procession in New York City. Chief Joseph accepted.

Erskine Wood, the son of Major Henry C. Wood, lived with the Nez Perce in Chief Joseph's teepee for five months during his thirteenth summer and for three months during his fourteenth summer, in 1892 and 1893. In a diary he kept of his experiences, he wrote:

> In all the time I was with Chief Joseph I never asked him or tried to talk to him about his campaign of 1877, the battles . . . the stratagems, the escapes, the long marches, and the final surrender. . . . It is probable Joseph would not have wanted to talk to me . . . even if we could have understood each other. It might have been too painful for him.[167]

So-ko-mop-o, a member of Chief Joseph's band, related that:

> I am ninety years old, perhaps more. . . . When Joseph and our people concluded to fight for his forefather's birthright, I was anxious to join him, but my husband protested against my engaging in hostilities against the whites. Regardless of his entreaties and objections, I joined Allocott and Joseph and went all through the campaign. I left my home and my husband to assist in the struggle, caused by the encroachment of the whites. . . . I am an aunt of Chief Joseph and I think him a brave, honest and fearless man who fought against overwhelming odds for the defence of his home and people.[168]

On June 30, 1895, Edward Latham, the Colville Agency physician, reported to the reservation agent, Captain John McAdam Webster:

> During the Winter Chief Joseph had a very severe case of Pneumonia and at first refused to be treated by me and I think would surely have died had it not been for Chief Peo who was visiting here. [h]e talked with him and the

> Nez Perces until he sent for me and after that I waited on him constantly for several weeks it was a hard fight but he recovered and since then I have had no trouble with his tribe. If any are sick and do not let me know, he comes himself and goes with me to see that the medicine is taken according to directions.[169]

Dr. Latham was also a serious photographer of the Nez Perce. His annoyance with a man who made his own terms is apparent in one of his letters to Edmond L. Meany of Seattle University:

> I got two negatives of Joseph. . . . The old rascal fixed himself in a horrible shape, no one would know that it was Joseph, he painted himself . . . dead black, was covered all with Eagle feathers, was riding a poor old bony horse he had. . . . The old scoundrel made me pay him ten dollars in advance, had I known how he was going to fix himself I would not have given him anything.[170]

7

PRODUCTION EMPHASIS

Applies pressure for productive output

From Henry's Lake to Bear Paw Mountains, all Howard could do was follow where the Indians led.[171]

Chief Joseph visited the Findley home during the development of the Findley–McNall dispute. One of A. B. Findley's children described the incident:

> Mother was preparing the evening meal and she chanced to look out the door and saw an Indian with the children who were playing in the yard. . . . Fearing they were in great danger, she quickly ran out. . . . She recognized the Indian as Chief Joseph, and her fears seemed to vanish. His friendly salutation reassured her and she returned to work and left the children with him.[172]

When Findley came in from the fields, they asked Chief Joseph to eat supper with them. He accepted the invitation. The Findley child continued:

> But soon began to ask Father questions about the difficulty on Whiskey Creek. Father thought it best to tell him all he could about it. . . . [He] probably unintentionally confirmed

> [Joseph's] belief that McNall was to blame for the Indian being killed.[173]

That Chief Joseph did not blame Findley was evidenced by the fact that Chief Joseph visited the family twice more that summer. "In these visits with Findley and other settlers, [he] seems to have been gathering evidence with a patience and sense of justice that would have done credit to the most learned of white investigators—had one been on the scene."[174]

In July 1877, the Battle of the Clearwater took place. Reports vary as to the number of casualties. Releases gave Howard's numbers as thirteen killed and twenty-two wounded. He calculated that Indian casualties included twenty-three killed, about forty wounded, and forty captured. Indian denials of these figures were emphatic. They claimed their casualties were four killed and six wounded.[175]

Joseph's people were still free after fighting to a standstill a force of supposedly well-trained soldiers of twice their number. General Howard, who had helped plan the battle of Gettysburg, said, "The Indians fought as well as any troops I ever saw . . . and so did ours, not onc man failing in duty."[176]

Second Lieutenant Charles E. S. Wood wrote: "It was a test case — all the hostiles under Joseph against all the soldiers under Howard."[177]

Just before starting the trek across the Lolo Trail in July 1877, the Nez Perce held a council to determine which direction they should take. Chief Joseph opposed flight of any kind.

He challenged the council members with:

> What are we fighting for? Is it for our lives? No! It is for this land where the bones of our fathers are buried. I do not want to take my women among strangers. I do not want to die in a strange land. Some of you tried to say, once, that I was afraid of the whites. Stay here with me now and you shall have plenty of fighting. We will put our women behind us in these mountains, and die in our own land fighting for them. I would rather do that than run I know not where.[178]

But by this time, the other chiefs were tired of fighting, and Chief Joseph deferred to the principle of united action. Looking Glass, who had often traveled over the one hundred fifty-mile-long Lolo Trail that led toward the plains, was unanimously voted headman for the journey. With that decision, the five bands became a single group of expatriate refugees.[179]

Chief Joseph described the meeting of the Army and the Nez Perce in Lolo Canyon in July 1877:

> Here another body of soldiers came upon us and demanded our surrender. We refused. They said, "You can not [*sic*] get by us." We answered, "We are going by you without fighting if you will let us, but we are going by you anyhow." We then made a treaty with these soldiers. We agreed not to molest anyone and they agreed that we might pass through the Bitter Root country in peace. We bought provisions and traded stock with the white men there.[180]

After the Battle of the Big Hole in August 1877, the Nez Perce prepared for flight while wounded children screamed with pain and women and children wailed for their dead. Chief Joseph superintended the moving, and Hohoto served as war leader in the place of Looking Glass, who had been temporarily demoted because of his failure to act upon wise suggestions for more haste and vigilance.[181]

In September 1877, the five bands camped near Cow Creek and found the Army unloading fifty tons of supplies from the steamer *Benton.* Two Nez Perce approached Sergeant William Molchert, in charge of the garrison at the Cow Island landing. They asked for food from the freight deposit that was to be shipped to outlying areas of the territory and offered to pay for it. At first Molchert refused, surprised that one Indian "spoke English as well as anyone could" and unhesitatingly expressed their friendship. He finally gave them a sack of hardtack and a side of bacon. He shook hands with the Nez Perce leader, whom he later declared was Joseph.[182] The bacon and hardtack were not enough for several hundred hungry people. Angered by this indifference, in the darkness the younger braves crept up to the freight piles and began looting the stores while other braves kept the soldiers and clerks of the trading companies barricaded behind a small earthwork. The braves appropriated all the food, tin ware, and other supplies they fancied. "We had privilege to do this," one of the braves reasoned. "It was war."[183] They also snitched four kegs of whiskey and promptly became drunk. Then they attempted at least three times to capture the soldiers guarding the supplies. Chief Joseph ordered the Indians to break up the barrels with axes. As the contents spilled from the broken barrels to the ground, one brave got down and lapped up the whiskey. Chief Joseph told him, "You will be shot if you get half shot."[184]

Word was passed around that Michael Foley sent a message to Fort Benton:

> Rifle Pit at Cow Island
> September 24, 1887—10 a.m.
>
> "Chief Joseph is here, and says he will surrender for two hundred bags of sugar. I told him to surrender without the sugar. He took the sugar and will not surrender. What will I do?"[185]

8

PREDICTIVE ACCURACY

Exhibits foresight and ability to predict outcomes accurately

---

We had many grievances,
but I knew that war would bring more.[186]

In 1875, two years before the Nez Perce retreat began, Chief Joseph strongly disagreed with the Nez Perce agency official about the proper way for an Indian to make a living.

Chief Joseph's "Dreamer Doctrine" of religion forbade all farming and all white ways. Its basic commandment was, "The Earth is our Mother; we must not wound her breast with plows and hoes."[187] They believed that to live fully, one must live with the land while neither changing nor damaging it.

While he probably did not accept these beliefs to the letter, Chief Joseph took delight in using them to annoy the agency officials. Besides which, he was understandably opposed to exchanging his herds of stock for a twenty-acre patch of land upon which to grow crops dictated by the agent. He must have wondered why, if stock raising was good for white men, it was not acceptable for Indians. It was obvious to Chief Joseph that if he moved to the reservation, the reduction of suitable range would correspondingly reduce the number of horses and cattle he could raise.

At Slate Creek, when Joseph learned the young men had been secretly buying large quantities of food and ammunition in the neighboring towns, he knew with certainty all his efforts, all his attempts at peace, were useless. After the surrender at Bear Paw, he said:

> I intended to go on the reservation. I knew nothing of these murders. Had I been home they would not have happened; but I was away on the other side of the Salmon River, killing some beef for my wife, who was sick, and I was called back by messengers telling me what the young men had done. Then I knew I must lead them in the fight, for the whites would not believe my story.[188]

In the predawn hours of August 9, 1877, at Big Hole Basin in Montana, the Army launched a surprise attack on the sleeping Nez Perce encampment. This was the first battle of the retreat in which the Nez Perce sustained severe losses. Several of their best fighting men died. Estimates indicate that twenty-five to fifty women and children were killed or wounded. After this battle, the Nez Perce changed their attitude and began to consider all whites—not just soldiers—as their enemies. Even now, however, the Nez Perce did not abuse captured women or scalp the dead.

Chief Joseph explained this humanitarian attitude:

> All the good Indians of their tribe held to communion with the spirits of their deceased friends.... These spirits frequently came to them in the still hours of the night . . . and gave them directions on what to do and how to live . . . such kind and humane treatment to the prisoners, had been in accordance with the directions of their spirit friends. That these spirits told them to always do what was right toward everyone; that they must stand up for what was right, and if they should be killed while so doing so, it would be all right with them. As the Indians expressed it, 'It would make no difference.'[189]

Just before the soldiers abandoned the Big Hole village, Two Moons, who was hiding at the creek, met Chief Joseph. As in earlier battles, Chief Joseph took no active part in the fighting. He had no gun, but he had been shielding his baby daughter, who had been born at Tepahlewan. Two Moons told Chief Joseph to "skip for your life. Without a gun you can do nothing. Save the child."[190]

Black Eagle reported Joseph's personal activities after the Battle of the Big Hole:

> Chief Joseph's horses with many others were on the open hillside to the west. The herd was back of and above the soldiers when they first charged the camp. I saw Chief Joseph and No Heart . . . going afoot after the horses. Both were barefooted, and Joseph had no leggings. Only shirt and blanket. Reaching their own horses, they mounted and drove the herd farther up the hill.[191]

This rescue of the horses "indicates Joseph's great presence of mind and ability to think and act in an emergency, for had Gibbon's men captured the herd of Indian ponies, the Nez Perces could have been defeated."[192]

After the battle of Big Hole, Chief Joseph said, "The Nez Perce never make war on women and children; we could have killed a great many . . . while the war lasted, but we would feel ashamed to do so."[193] Chief Joseph felt a very real sense of shame in killing anyone. He had opposed it on moral grounds, and the knowledge of a future in which his people would have to kill to stay alive haunted him. He would continue to move on grimly with the others, seemingly numb at times. But the savagery of the attack at Big Hole and the wanton slaughter of women and children had confirmed his worst fears about the war.

The Canyon Creek fight took place on September 13, 1877. The Nez Perce accompanying Joseph later brought to light that afterward Chief Joseph became more authoritative and his assertiveness increased markedly as the band left the army behind and became more confident they would make good their escape to Canada. It was also after the Canyon Creek fight that the Nez Perce learned the futility of depending upon the Crows for assistance in their flight. On

September 14 and 15, the Crows attacked the Nez Perce. Theodore Goldin, one of the troopers, witnessed the results:

> The Crows had come up with a considerable body of the enemy and were hotly engaging them near the edge of a belt of timber. . . . As we watched . . . we were surprised to see the Nez Perces ride out of the timber in almost perfect line of battle formation; there were possibly a couple of hundred of them and for some distance they moved forward in what appeared to be perfect alignment, then the two flanks opened out into a perfect skirmish line with the seeming purpose of flanking the Crows. This style of fighting was too much for our allies; they couldn't understand it, and as practically all of them were young warriors, they fired a few hasty shots and then broke and fell back in great confusion. In fact by far the larger part of them kept on falling back until they reached the reservation miles away.[194]

After leaving Cow Island, the Nez Perce traveled to Cow Creek Canyon, where they skirmished with the soldiers on September 25, 1877. The exhausted bands, moving slowly, then headed north and slightly west to the Bear Paw Mountains. They set up camp along Snake Creek, a hard day's march from Canada, intending to rest, recuperate, and hunt. Chief Joseph later said:

> I sat down in a fat and beautiful country. I had won my freedom and the freedom of my people. There were many empty places in the lodges . . . but we were in the land where we would not be forced to live in a place we did not want. I believed that if I could remain safe at a distance and talk straight to the men that would be sent by the Great Father, I could get back the Wallowa Valley and return in peace. That is why I did not allow my young men to kill and destroy the white settlers after I began to fight. I wanted to leave a clean trail, and if there were dead soldiers in that trail I could not be held to blame.[195]

In the post-surrender days, following an interview with Chief Joseph, newspaper correspondent Thomas Sutherland wrote:

> Gen Howard and Col. Miles had several talks with Joseph. He stated his losses and revealed his actions very freely. He reiterated that he was across the Salmon River when the war began; said he knew nothing of the murders on Camas Prairie; that the murderers were now dead; says his wife was sick [confined] at the time of the outbreak.[196]

When Joseph was asked where he got his military expertise, he replied: "The Great Spirit puts it in the heart and head of man to know how to defend himself." He admitted, however, that he and his people had learned to maneuver by watching the cavalry in their daily drills. This sharp observation, wisely applied, enabled the Nez Perce to use all the military tactics the white soldiers employed. In each engagement, the Chief knew accurately the number of troops opposing him until the final battle. At Bear Paw the chiefs neglected to send out scouts or post sentinels around the camp as they had done all times previously. Had the Indians spread a chain of scouts, they might have avoided the last fight.[197]

The Nez Perce had left Idaho in June with approximately 750 people. The group included women and children, the sick and old, all their baggage, and their extensive horse herd. At Bear Paw Mountain, 418 people surrendered with Chief Joseph. A large proportion of the men were elderly, and some forty were wounded. The Nez Perce interpreter counted 1,531 horses, 300 saddles, bridles, ropes, camp equipment, and blankets surrendered. The Nez Perces understood that 700 horses would be returned to them.[198]

When Chief Joseph surrendered that day, it was with General Miles' assurance of "no more battles and blood. From this sun we will have a good time on both sides, your band and mine."[199] Miles explained that the plan was for the Nez Perce to go to Fort Keogh for the winter and then return to the Lapwai reservation in the spring. General Miles had won the confidence of the Nez Perce, so much so that they regarded him as their protector and surrendered their arms to him. Yellow Wolf expressed their feelings when he said, "Now we understand these words, and will go with General Miles. He is head man. We will go with him."[200]

In a matter of weeks, General Howard's superiors overruled the surrender terms he and Miles had made with Chief Joseph. Miles explained it to Chief Joseph:

> You must not blame me. I have endeavored to keep my word, but the chief who is over me has given the order and I must obey it or resign. That would do you no good. Some other officer would carry out the order.[201]

Chief Joseph believed Miles and did not blame him, but he later remarked about the federal system and its political and military hierarchy, "White men have too many chiefs."[202]

9

TOLERANCE OF FREEDOM

Allows followers scope for initiative, decision, and action

A war is a thing where there are two sides.[203]

In May 1877, several young Nez Perce warriors—who were not of Joseph's band—attacked and killed some settlers. In mistaken retribution, angry settlers fired upon Joseph's people, who were on their way to the reservation as ordered, but who had temporarily encamped with several other Nez Perce bands. Because of this sequence of events, Joseph decided to join up with the bands refusing to go to the reservation and led his people to White Bird Creek in Idaho.

Joseph later said:

> I know that my young men did a great wrong, but I ask, Who was first to blame? They had been insulted a thousand times; their fathers and brothers had been killed; their mothers and wives had been disgraced; they had been driven to madness by the whiskey sold to them by white men . . . and added to all this, they were homeless and desperate.[204]

Major Henry Wood wrote a letter to the *Army and Navy Journal* concerning the attack:

> An officer of sound judgment and with a good opportunity for ascertaining facts writes me as follows, viz: . . . during all this time and for some days before, it is known Joseph and his brother were over on the Salmon River, curing or jerking beef for their families, and returned on the evening of the 14th to hear *for the first time* of the Outbreak; and Joseph proposed to go at once to the Agency and give himself up, but was persuaded by his . . . brother not to do so. They then went over to White Bird's camp and had a talk, Joseph being urged on by the others, although none of his band had been implicated up to that time. That night, however, a few of his men, who had some grudge against Norton, living on Cottonwood Creek, started off to kill him. . . . It is said that Joseph, on learning of this, said it was too late to turn back, or words to that effect, and that he would cast his lot or take chances with the rest. . . . It is my belief that Joseph was urged into this war against his judgment and inclination, and would gladly be well out of it.[205]

John W. Houston, Attorney General for Idaho, wrote to the U. S. Attorney General:

> The massacres on Camas Prairie Salmon River and White Bird Creek in June last and which were the initatiory [*sic*] steps to the general outbreak by Joseph's band were committed by a few Indians belonging to the band but were not I am satisfied from all the evidence I have been able to procure either advised or sanctioned by Chief Joseph.[206]

The attack by the Army on Looking Glass's camp at Clear Creek took place on July 1, 1877. Captain Stephen Whipple's report stated that "an opportunity was given Looking Glass to surrender, which he at first promised to accept, but afterward defiantly refused, and the result was that several Indians were killed."[207]

The Nez Perce, however, said Looking Glass did not promise to meet with the soldiers, that he sent a messenger to warn Whipple and his men not to cross the creek to the village. Whipple and several others ignored this advice and crossed the creek anyway. One of the soldiers fired at and struck one of the Indians in the village, thus precipitating the battle. Prior to this confrontation, Looking Glass had adamantly rejected participation in any part of the war, and believed that the whites knew and understood his position. This attack ultimately provided strong impetus for him to join his forces with those of Chief Joseph.[208]

After the Clearwater battle in July 1877, Chief Joseph, under a flag of truce, sent a message to General Howard asking for the terms under which the Nez Perce could surrender.

Lieutenant Wood, General Howard's aide, said that he was informed long afterward by an Indian living in the area that "Joseph wished to surrender rather than leave the country or bring further misery on his people, but that, in council, he was overpowered by others, especially Looking Glass,"[209] and that he would not desert the common cause. The decision of the chiefs to cross the Salmon River and await the arrival of General Howard was in line with Joseph's reluctance to leave the Nez Perce homeland.[210]

After the battle of the Big Hole in August 1877, General Howard reported that the Nez Perce had lost eighty-nine people in the fight. The Indians themselves explained the numbers more precisely: Only twelve of their fighting men were lost in that battle, and the rest of the dead were women, children, and old men.[211] The killing of non-warriors appalled the Nez Perce because, except for the Slate Creek raid, they had fought according to the white man's army code of Civil War days.

In 1889, twelve years after the final surrender at the Bear Paw Mountains, Chief Joseph visited New York City and stayed at the Astor House. One of the women guests, who was wearing a hat decorated with an incredible array of birds and flowers, asked Chief Joseph if he had ever scalped anyone. Chief Joseph thought carefully before turning to his interpreter. Indicating the woman's hat, Chief Joseph said quietly, "Tell her I have nothing in my collection as fine as that."[212]

During this same visit, Chief Joseph said during an interview:

> This East is strange to me. I do not understand it at all. The green of the trees and the grass is not here. The quiet

> of the woods is missing. It is all dirt and noise and hurry and the people are strange. I notice many things as I walk, and they puzzle me. The white men have put up buildings which one cannot see the top of. They tell me people stay there and labor during the day. I have had white men who know the ways of their fellows tell me many strange things. I can understand a little English myself, but I cannot speak any. The white men are very wonderful and skilful [*sic*], to do some of these things. They send the cars along on a rope [trolley cars] and the buildings up into the sky. They have railroads in the air [the elevated trains], and they go up and down the buildings [elevators] without moving themselves. I have heard much of these wonders in Washington, and one or two of them I saw in Portland once. But here in New York it is all wonders, and I do not understand how the people live. It is good for me to see these things before I die, and so I must see them now, for I do not expect to leave my people for so long again.[213]

Chief Joseph ended this trip to New York City as he did so many other things—on his own terms while allowing others to be themselves. He had been invited to a dinner. When his host, G. O. Shields, called for him at his hotel, the clerk informed Mr. Shields that Chief Joseph was not there any longer, that he had left the morning before.

Mr. Shields, bewildered, told the clerk that Chief Joseph had been scheduled to stay through the week and attend the Camp Fire Club dinner.

The clerk replied, "Yes, but Chief Joseph said he wanted to get where he could see some trees."[214]

10

CONSIDERATION

Regards the comfort, well-being, status, and contributions of followers

The campaign could only be won by the pervading influence and leadership of an exceptional character.[215]

Chief Joseph was, apparently, preparing his people for war a full year before it began. At the trading post in Lewiston, Idaho, the Nez Perce women were seen buying large amounts of flour and other supplies, as for a lengthy campaign. The observers failed to realize that Joseph simply did not know what was ahead for his people and so was preparing for any possibility.

Continued flight was the only strategy possible for the Nez Perce after the battle of Big Hole, and this decision reflects Chief Joseph's increasing influence. Even while he had been the foremost champion of non-treaty Nez Perce rights, at the same time he abhorred the outbreak of war and took up the campaign reluctantly. He had favored fighting in Idaho, but Looking Glass's decision to retreat to Crow territory had been approved by the Indian council. After the battle of Big Hole, Looking Glass's popularity declined and Chief Joseph's rose because

> [he] had demonstrated an unwavering concern for the well-being of all the people. . . . His sense of responsibility encompassed them all. He possessed an inherent

> understanding of their hardships and suffering that constantly enlarged his stature as the guardian of the people.[216]

One story told after the battle of the Big Hole concerns an elder, Black Tail, distinguished as the most well-to-do member of the Nez Perce tribe. Black Tail apparently had six thousand dollars in twenty-dollar gold pieces that he carried in a buckskin bag. One of the officers who took part in the Bear Paw battle wrote:

> Many of the Indians have money, one old aristocrat having $6,000 in gold. The old chap says that he lost it in the battle of the Big Hole, and being near-sighted could not find it. Its loss so worried him that Joseph after a few days sent the old man with two young men back, and, after a few days' search, found it.[217]

When the Nez Perce, still heading north, left Cow Island, they were less than eighty miles from Canada. On September 24, 1877, they camped near O. G. Cooper's freighter train. Cooper's observation of them in those last days before they reached Snake Creek and the Bear Paw Mountains is a telling one:

> There were between seven and eight hundred men, women, and children, perhaps more . . . and I should judge about four hundred warriors . . . all the young sprightly bucks had but a few cartridges in their belts, while the old fellows, and the middle-aged, seemed better supplied. . . . They had but a few lodges with them. . . . Their animals were very poor, and many had sore backs and feet, but they had some fine horses with them. . . . About twenty of their horses, crippled and dead, were left along Cow Creek.[218]

During the initial surrender discussions at Bear Paw Mountain, Chief Joseph was hoping that some of his men had escaped to get help from Sitting Bull in Canada and would return with reinforcements. After he realized that Sitting Bull was not going to help him, and that further resistance was useless, he decided to surrender because: "I could not bear to see my wounded men and women suffer any longer; we had lost enough already. . . . I thought we could start again."[219]

On October 5, 1877, Joseph surrendered the remnants of his band—eighty-seven men, one hundred eighty-four women, one hundred forty-seven children[220]—to General Howard. Before he did so, Chief Joseph argued with Looking Glass, who told Chief Joseph that he had had his experiences with a man of two faces and two tongues. If Joseph surrendered, he (Joseph) would be sorry and in his sorrow he would rather be dead, than suffer such deception.

Joseph replied that many of their people were out on the hills naked and freezing. The women were suffering with cold, the children crying with the chilly dampness of the shelter pits. "For myself I do not care. It is for them I am going to surrender."[221]

Of the Bear Paw Mountain defeat, Chief Joseph later said they could have escaped from the Bear Paw if they had left their wounded, old women, and children behind. "We were unwilling to do this. We never heard of a wounded Indian recovering while in the hands of white men."[222]

He then related that during the flight to Canada, Howard's scouts had killed and scalped all the aged or wounded Nez Perce left behind on the trail when it had become impossible for them to keep up with the band any longer.[223] Chief Joseph also spoke of how Howard's scouts had dug up the Nez Perce dead and scalped them.

As the Nez Perce leaders held a final council before the surrender, General Miles sent a message asking to speak directly to Chief Joseph. The leaders decided Joseph should meet with Miles. All who wanted to surrender took their guns to General Miles and gave them up. Those who did not want to surrender kept their guns. The surrender was just for those who did not longer want to fight. Joseph spoke only for his own band, what they wanted to do.[224] Thus, when Chief Joseph surrendered, he clearly established his intention to surrender his own band and himself; he would leave to someone else the decision of the futures of the other bands. As it happened, after Chief Joseph gave up his rifle that October afternoon, other groups of Nez Perce, at different times as each decided that giving themselves up was the only choice, left the earthworks and turned over their weapons to the army officers. An onlooker wrote:

> The other chiefs and their companions who had followed Joseph into the camp performed the same ceremony. . . . In reversing their weapons [they] gave significance to the act easily appreciated by the veterans who were silent witnesses of it.[225]

Because all of the Indians had not surrendered by nightfall, the soldiers were ordered to keep night watch against the "hostiles." Despite this small detail, General Miles jumped the gun, as it were, and wrote to General Terry:

> We have had our usual success. We made a very direct and rapid march across the country, and after a severe engagement, and being kept under fire for three [*sic*] days, the hostile camp of Nez Perces, under Chief Joseph, surrendered at two o'clock to-day.[226]

Following the surrender, Chief Joseph acknowledged:

> General Miles had promised that we might return to our country with what stock we had left. . . . I believed General Miles, or *I never would have surrendered.*[227]

After the surrender at Bear Paw, Chief Joseph's care and concern for his people drew respect from both Indians and white men. In the Benton *Record* for October 12, 1877, J. J. Healy reported that "Joseph was walking round about his people talking to the wounded and occasionally addressing the warriors by signs and seemed quite unconcerned about his defeat." Healy observed that the people "quickly responded to his leadership."[228]

When the Nez Perce were consigned to Fort Leavenworth, Kansas, in November 1877, their camp was placed between a swampy slough and the Missouri River. Between December 4, 1877 and July 1878, twenty-one Indians died. Chief Joseph pleaded with the government to either return the Nez Perce to Idaho or let them select land in the Indian Territory. General Sherman disapproved the petition because "the Nez Perces should be handled and located at the convenience of the government, without reference to their desires."[229]

In later years, recalling the desolation of Fort Leavenworth, Chief Joseph said, "The Great Spirit Chief who rules above seemed to be looking the other way and did not see what was being done to my people."[230]

Erskine Wood, Chief Joseph's summer guest for two years, wrote:

> He was the kindest of fathers to me, looking after me, providing for me, caring for me, and, it must be said, sometimes gently rebuking me when necessary. . . . Joseph, himself, made me a bonnet out of muskrat fur, with a big eagle feather standing upright, and little red medallions cut out of blanket sewed against the fur. One instance of his care for me, among many, is the diary entry for Monday, November 6, where he, observing how tired I was from the day before, bade me not hunt that day, but stay in the teepee and rest.[231]

Erskine Wood also noted that while he was staying with Chief Joseph, Niky Mowitz and Erskine became good friends. Niky was Chief Joseph's nephew. Chief Joseph had adopted him after Niky's own father was killed during the Nez Perce flight. This "speaks eloquently for Joseph's inherently humane nature [*sic*] and for his grief over the loss of his own four sons."[232]

In 1904, Chief Joseph visited the University of Washington in Seattle. After giving a short talk before the students, Chief Joseph attended a football game:

> He followed the plays with deep absorption, and excitedly got to his feet to watch intently whenever the players would pile up in scrimmage after being tackled. Then, when they untangled themselves, he would draw a long breath and sit down again.[233]

In a newspaper article in the *Oregon Sunday Journal* on Christmas Day 1904, Edward Latham, the reservation physician, was quoted:

> For years I had befriended Joseph and nursed him as if he were a child when he had pneumonia, and had fed him from my cellar when he was in need of food. Knowing this I thought there would be little trouble in inducing Joseph to pose for a photograph. Joseph demurred. There is no use hurrying an Indian. Some days later I mentioned it again. He refused flatly. Winter came on. He got out of food. I gave him a sack of potatoes and mentioned the picture. I gave him another sack of potatoes 2 weeks later and again I mentioned the picture. He said, "Sometime" . . . Then I gave him 2 sacks of potatoes and $5. He promised to dress in all his regalia and go to some wild spot on the river and pose for the picture. On the first pretty day, the time agreed upon for taking the picture, I appeared, camera in hand, but Joseph didn't even grunt. I appealed to his [wives]. One began jabbering and going for him . . . I heard her mention the potatoes several times over. Then he got up and said "All right", and the picture here given was the result.[234]

Although Chief Joseph ruled the men, he apparently did not always have the final say in his household, if one can judge by his statement that "when you can get the last word with an echo, you may have the last word with your wife."[235]

11

TOLERANCE OF UNCERTAINTY

Able to tolerate uncertainty and postponement without anxiety or upset

---

Within the limits of the reservation he lived his life quietly with a calm and dignified acceptance of his fate.[236]

During the initial surrender discussions, Chief Joseph sent as his representative a sub-chief, Yellow Bull, to meet with General Miles's representative under a flag of truce. Chief Joseph later described Yellow Bull's efforts:

> General Miles would not let me leave the tent to see my friend alone. Yellow Bull said to me: "They have got you in their power and I am afraid they will never let you go again. I have an officer in our camp [Second Lieutenant Lovell H. Jerome], and I will hold him until they let you go free."
>
> I said: "I do not know what they mean to do with me, but if they kill me, you must not kill the officer. It will do no good to avenge my death by killing him."[237]

Chief Joseph later said of his interview:

> Yellow Bull understood the messenger to say that General Miles wished me to consider the situation; that he did not want to kill my people unnecessarily. Yellow Bull understood

> this to be a demand for me to surrender and save blood. Upon reporting this message to me Yellow Bull said he wondered whether General Miles was in earnest. I sent him back with my answer, that I had not made up my mind, but would think about it and send word soon. A little later he sent some Cheyenne scouts with another message. I went out to meet them. They said they believed General Miles was sincere and really wanted peace. I walked on to General Miles's tent. He met me and we shook hands. He said, "Come, let us sit down by the fire and talk this matter over."[238]

Major Henry R. Tilton, the Army's chief surgeon, described Chief Joseph as he walked over to General Miles's tent: "A young man of fine presence. He appeared very sad. . . . He said they were short of rations and could not move without their ponies." [239]

Chief Joseph told Miles that although he himself was willing to surrender, many of the others did not share his opinion and were strongly opposed to it. When Miles insisted Joseph must turn over all the weapons among the Nez Perce, Joseph requested that they be permitted to keep half their weapons in order to hunt game.[240]

Thus, Chief Joseph, on his own time and terms, began the negotiations that ended the "last serious Indian disturbance in the Pacific Northwest."[241]

Tom Hill, a mixed-blood Nez Perce with Delaware ancestry, explained the sequence of events after the discussion between Miles and Chief Joseph:

> Joseph . . . started to the camp, but Miles told me to remain. [He] had gone only about twenty-five yards, when Miles told me to call Joseph back. When the chief came back, the General sent me over to the camp and kept Joseph.[242]

The following morning, Lieutenant Jerome and Chief Joseph were exchanged. Jerome later described his experience:

> On that day [October 1] I received a message from Miles early in the forenoon [*sic*]. Miles evidently wanted to keep

> Joseph, but wanted me to escape. I believe now that if I had not gone into that camp under the General's order, he, being deprived of the information which I gave him afterward, would have withdrawn—holding Joseph as his prisoner—with his force to the cover of the distant woods, and there entrenched himself. . . . He was very anxious . . . lest Sitting Bull should come to the Nez Perces' assistance. . . . While I was in their camp, several warriors spoke of this matter.[243]

Lieutenant Jerome described the exchange itself:

> There were three Indians along with me. I suppose that was an interesting position. With the suspicion of treachery on both sides, thirteen of our men lay in their trenches scarcely forty rods off, with the rifles held at a dead rest on Joseph and my three Indian guards. More than twenty Indians had an equally sure sight over their Winchester's and Henry's [*sic*] straight at General Miles and me. I have since learned that Miles' staff officer held a cocked revolver in his bosom ready to fix Joseph if I should be harmed. The transfer passed without trouble, and I was restored to the command of my company.[244]

Miles's action was

> A clear affront to the Nez Perces as well as a direct violation of the concept of truce. . . . But in his quest for victory, he likely rationalized that the unconventional nature of warfare with Indians gave him license to disregard formality, despite the obvious duplicity of his actions.[245]

True to his pledge, Chief Joseph fought no longer, although he continued working for the betterment of his people and for his dream that they would one day be allowed to return to the Wallowa Valley where the bones of their ancestors were.

In March 1879, Chief Joseph visited President Hayes in Washington. He described his political contacts:

> I have seen the Great Father Chief (the President); the next Great Chief (Secretary of the Interior); the Commissioner Chief (Hayt); the Law Chief (General Butler); and many other law chiefs (congressmen), and they all say they are my friends, and that I shall have justice.[246]

During this visit, Chief Joseph revealed:

> We were moved from Baxter Springs [Kansas] to the Indian Territory, and set down without our lodges. We had but little medicine, and we were nearly all sick. Seventy of my people have died since we moved there.[247]

Chief Joseph told a reporter of the *North American Review:*

> I have heard talk and talk, but nothing is done. Good words do not last long until they amount to something. Words do not pay for my dead people. They do not pay for my country, now overrun by white men. They do not protect my father's grave. They do not pay for my horses and cattle. Good words will not give me back my children. . . . Good words will not give my people good health and stop them from dying. Good words will not get my people a home where they can live in peace and take care of themselves.[248]

In 1879, Chief Joseph traveled to Washington to plead his cause before President Hayes. While there, the *North American Review* interviewed him on his life. This account was published in April 1879 and titled "An Indian's Views of Indian Affairs." In it Chief Joseph said:

> I know that my race must change. We cannot hold our own with the white men as we are. We only ask an even chance to live as other men live. We ask to be recognized as men. We ask that the same law shall work alike on all men. . . . Let me be a free man—free to travel, free to stop, free to work, free to trade, where I choose, free to choose my own teachers, free to follow the religion of my fathers, free

> to think and talk and act for myself—and I will obey every law, or submit to the penalty.[249]

Some of the settlers wanted nothing to do with the Indians, but some became fond of Chief Joseph and a few of them grew to think of him as a good, trusted friend. During his interview for the *North American Review* of April 1879, Chief Joseph said:

> I have carried a heavy load on my back ever since I was a boy. I learned then that we were but few, while the white men were many, and that we could not hold our own with them. We were like deer. They were like grizzly bears. We had a small country. Their country was large. We were contented to let things remain as the Great Spirit Chief made them. They were not; and would change the rivers and mountains if they did not suit them.
>
> If the white man wants to live in peace with the Indian he can live in peace. There need be no trouble. Treat all men alike. . . . Give them all an even chance to live and grow. All men were made by the same Great Spirit Chief. They are all brothers. The earth is the mother of all people, and all people should have equal rights upon it. You might as well expect the rivers to run backward as that any man who was born a free man should be contented penned up and denied liberty to go where he pleases. If you tie a horse to a stake, do you expect he will grow fat? If you pen an Indian up on a small spot of earth and compel him to stay there, he will not be contented—nor will he grow and prosper. I have asked some of the great white chiefs where they get their authority to say to the Indian that he shall stay in one place, while he sees white men going where they please. They cannot tell me.
>
> I only ask of the Government to be treated as all other men are treated. If I cannot go to my own home, let me have a home in some country where my people will not die so fast. I would like to go to Bitter Root Valley. There my people would be healthy; where they are now they are dying. Three have died since I left my camp to come to Washington.[250]

In the spring of 1889, the land allotment for the Nez Perce on the Lapwai Reservation began. Alice Fletcher, in charge of the division process, and E. Jane Gay, her assistant who was also the project's photographer, spent twenty-nine months surveying the Nez Perce Reservation and assigning land portions to individual members of the tribe.[251]

Jane Gay was apparently not impressed by the abilities of the Nez Perce when it came to hard work. She wrote:

> They can ride ponies all day, but walking is a new sensation. Their leg muscles are flabby and sharp stones cut moccasined feet. . . . The poor fellows succumb crossing a canyon of only half pitch and they faint on the mountains when the thermometer is only 110 in the shade.

In light of this viewpoint, Miss Gay's assessment of Chief Joseph is revealing:

> It was good to see an unsubjugated Indian. . . . He cannot be persuaded to take his land upon the Reservation. He will have none but the Wallowa Valley, from which he was driven; he will remain landless and homeless if he cannot have his own again. . . . One could not help respecting the man who still stood firmly for his rights, after having fought and suffered and been defeated in the struggle for their maintenance.[252]

When Alice Fletcher and E. Jane Gay had completed the project, they had made 2,009 allotments totaling 175,026 acres to the Nez Perce.[253]

On August 24, 1900, Chief Joseph wrote to Professor Edmond L. Meany of Seattle University, Washington:

> I have just returned from Wallowa where I went . . . to look over my old home and see if I could find a new home now. There are many white people there now, but I told the inspector I would be satisfied with some land on one side

> of the river where there were only a few whites, and where creeks and mountains afforded good pasturage. I would be happy with very little. You would be very welcome here. I would be glad to see you. A long time ago we were not friends to the white people but we are friends now. . . . My father, mother and brother are buried at Wallowa and when I die I want to be buried there.[254]

On May 27, 1901, Chief Joseph wrote to Meany:

> The children of my people are attending the Day School on the Reservation. . . . This land belonged to the late Chief Moses. It does not belong to me. My old home is in the Wallowa Valley and I want to go back there to live.[255]

On November 11, 1903, Chief Joseph addressed the students at the University of Washington:

> It always gives me pleasure to meet my white friends. I seem to have so many more now, than during my younger life. . . . I was born and reared [to lead] the free, open and unrestricted life of a brave and haughty warrior. When I reached manhood I found that conditions were rapidly changing and without going into details, fought for my people, my land and my home. I fought for the inheritance left me by my forefathers and given me by [the Creator]. I was vanquished, conquered and subjugated, and have keenly felt the humiliation of defeat. But I have come to fully realize the kindness and generosity of the whites. I now see that they are my friends. In my declining years, I long to return to my old home in Wallowa Valley, where most of my relatives and friends are sleeping their last sleep. I have repeatedly petitioned the Great Father in Washington to transfer my self [*sic*] and small band to our old home, that we may die in the country, having so many tender memories. . . . To return to Wallowa Valley, is a wish I Cherish very dearly. That is all.[256]

Following his death, Chief Joseph was quietly buried at Nespelem, but on June 20, 1905, he was "reburied" and a monument erected to his memory. Yellow Bull spoke during the ceremony:

> I am glad to see our white friends here attending this ceremony, and it seems . . . we all have the same sad feelings, and [this should] wipe [away] my tears. Joseph is dead, but his words are not dead; his words will live forever. This monument will stand—and Joseph's words will stand as long as this monument.[257]

Twenty-one years after Chief Joseph's death, one hundred Nez Perce received permission to dig up the bones of Old Chief Joseph and re-inter them on the shore of Wallowa Lake. Two thousand white people attended the ceremony in which the bones were reburied beneath a granite column.

The honors bestowed on Chief Joseph in his late years and since his death cannot atone for the deceit, the broken promises, the bloody war forced upon him during his lifetime. In *Builders of the Northwest*, Jalmar Johnson asks, "Who was the savage and who the civilized in the white man's conquest of the red man's America? In the case of Chief Joseph, the answer is obvious."[258]

Howard, in *Saga of Chief Joseph*, says of the honors he received: "All of which recognition the chief would have gladly exchanged for the privilege of living and dying in his beloved Wallowa—the valley of winding waters."[259]

Erskine Wood's second summer visit with Chief Joseph was in 1893. At their final departure, Joseph charged the young white boy to "Be brave and tell the truth." It was a command that Erskine Wood carried throughout his life in his personal fight for justice and truth.[260]

Chief Joseph's likeness is carved into the white marble shaft that marks his grave. Facing southwest toward the Wallowa Valley of Oregon, he looks eternally upon the land he spent his lifetime trying to recover.

In October 1907, James McLaughlin, the Indian Agent who had made the final decision that the Nez Perce should not be allowed to return to the Wallowa Valley, visited the Bear Paw battlefield. He reported:

> The battlefield is wholly neglected. It presents no other proof of the fact that it was the scene of one of the decisive battles of the Indian wars, except the disturbed face of the ground where the rifle-pits were dug, and a yawning trench, some thirty feet long and six feet wide, where the fallen soldiers were hastily buried. . . . In a few years the roller of time will have utterly removed even these evidences of the past.[261]

In 1929 the Daughters of the American Revolution placed a memorial on the site dedicated to the soldiers who were killed there. In 1930 Congress passed legislation authorizing a marker on the battlefield. In September 1931, Congress sanctioned a monument consisting of an eight-ton rock with a bronze plaque. In the late 1920s and mid-1930s, Nez Perce warriors who had survived and white civilians marked localized places on the battlefield, helping to preserve its historical integrity while enhancing its potential for interpretation. Thus Bear Paw became "one of the best preserved Indian wars battlefields in the country, commensurate with its importance in American history."[262]

In 1902, a woman from Spokane, who was making a bas-relief of Chief Joseph from a photograph taken of him as a young man, visited Nespelem. She showed Chief Joseph the picture. After gazing upon it for a long moment, he said quietly, "That man died long ago."[263]

12
REPRESENTATION

Speaks and acts as representative of the group

The surrender speech confirmed Joseph in the public's mind as the symbol of the Nez Perces' heroic, fighting retreat.[264]

Chief Joseph was born in 1840 in a cave near the mouth of present-day Joseph Creek in the Wallowa country.[265] Tu-eka-kas, his father, was chief of the Wellamotkin band of Chute-pa-lu—the Nez Perce. His mother was Khapkhaponimi (Loose Bark on Trees). He had two older sisters, Celia and Elawinonmi, and two younger brothers, Shugun (Brown) and Ollicut (Frog).[266]

Chief Joseph, a traditionally educated Nez Perce, sought his answers from Mother Earth, as when he explained the religious feelings of the young men who would not work the land after they were consigned to the Reservation: "The earth and myself are of one mind. The measure of the land and the measure of our bodies are the same."[267]

For years, Agent Monteith argued that the Indian Agent should have more power over the Nez Perce. Before the Nez Perce decision to flee to Canada, Monteith stated, "I have given Joseph until April 1, 1877 to come on the reservation peaceably. *They can come at one time just as well as at another, having nothing to hinder them in moving.*"[268]

Monteith had lived in the Wallowa country for six years at this time and knew the potential of the Snake River to flood from April to July. He also knew the Nez Perce practice of permitting their stock to range freely to sheltered canyons and valleys in the winter, where the spring crop of colts and calves was dropped in April and May. An early roundup would be difficult to accomplish in melting snow and spring rains. The mares and colts, the cows and calves, needed at least two to three months to be strong enough to swim the rivers. Thus, mid-July was not an unreasonable time for the Nez Perce to leave. Monteith, however, decreed that "if he [Joseph] is allowed to have his own way at this time, it will only make him more stubborn in the future."[269]

During the Findley/McNall trouble, Chief Joseph explained that two settlers had boasted that if he did not behave, all the Indians would be killed. Chief Joseph would be killed and scalped by Cochran (or King) and Cochran (or King) would wear his scalp as a bridle. When Cochran and King were confronted by seventy angry braves, stripped and painted for war at the ranch where they were staying, Cochran hid under a haystack in the barn. King crawled under a bed inside the house. When the Indians demanded they appear, the one in the barn was dragged out by other settlers, and a woman went to get the one hidden under the bed. All the settlers were angry with the two men for bragging as they had. The woman stood in the bedroom doorway and cried: "You come out of thar or I'll come in and drag you out. We wouldn't be having all this trouble and scare if you had kept your big mouth shut and not bragged so much."[270]

Chief Joseph, holding a long club over the man who had been dragged from the barn, demanded to know whether these were the men who had been bragging about scalping him. The man's father then told Chief Joseph that he would take Cochran out of the country at once if Chief Joseph would let him go. Chief Joseph agreed, and the father took his son away, keeping him out of the valley as long as Chief Joseph remained there. "Thus once again the good judgment and goodwill of Joseph and the Nez Perces prevented a violent response under great provocation."[271]

Before the May 1877 council at Lapwai, Chief Joseph had been keeping in touch with the developments taking place. He was able to keep the younger Indians from acting rashly that spring, but he was concerned about the future. He sent word to General Howard requesting a personal interview as soon as possible. Chief Joseph was afraid that the Fort Lapwai interpreter the previous fall had not translated accurately and it was vitally important that the Indians know exactly what they were expected to do that spring.[272]

In July 1877, during the Nez Perce flight to Canada, the public began to criticize General Howard and to give grudging praise to the Nez Perce and especially to Chief Joseph who was, supposedly, leading them. General Howard had already figured out that he was fighting a shrewd, intelligent strategist, but the public began to realize that the Indians had fooled the Army several times and accorded this action to Chief Joseph. Fair-minded settlers at Slate Creek and other places where conflict had taken place pointed out that the Nez Perce had been conducting themselves in a manner unusual for "Indians on the warpath" in that they did not scalp or mutilate bodies, treated white women and non-combatants with humanity and friendliness and otherwise adhered to the white man's code of war. The Nez Perce warriors giving money to the Slate Creek settlers to pay for the damage they had inflicted was considered unprecedented and was credited to Chief Joseph, whose dignity and decency at prewar councils was remembered by those who had attended them.

After the surrender, the Nez Perce were sent to Fort Keogh, near Miles City, Montana, but Sheridan immediately sent them on to Fort Lincoln at Bismark, Dakota Territory. When they reached Bismark, the townspeople, mirroring the respect and admiration of the nation for their courage during their ill-fated flight, treated them like heroes. A special dinner was held for Chief Joseph, and he received this invitation, later printed in the Bismarck *Tri-Weekly Tribune* on November 21, 1877:

> Bismark, D. T., Nov. 21, 1877. To Joseph, Head Chief of the Nez Perces. Sir: —Desiring to show you our kind feelings and the admiration we have for your bravery and humanity, as exhibited in your recent conflict with the forces of the United States, we most cordially invite you to dine with us at the Sheridan House, in this city. The dinner to be given at 1 1/2 p.m. today.[273]

Joseph and other chiefs also held a reception at the Sheridan, where he was presented to a number of the ladies of the house. He was served salmon at the dinner and, it was later reported, said that it reminded him of his own country.[274]

Even when he was not physically present, Chief Joseph maintained a position of leadership among the Nez Perce. When an army delegation traveled to Canada to attempt to get White Bird and his people to return to the United States, Chief Joseph was used as "bait" to persuade them. Lieutenant George W. Baird "lied outright to White Bird," telling him:

> If you on this side of the line, wish to go to Joseph, you will be treated just as well and have the same protection as Joseph and his people. Joseph and his Indians will be put on a good Reservation, and have an opportunity to live comfortably.[275]

After the Nez Perce were consigned to the reservation, Monteith's ideas included forbidding any of the Indians from going buffalo hunting or camas gathering. He insisted the Indian horse herds should be confiscated so that the Nez Perce would have to take up day labor to earn spending money. He argued that children should be taken from their parents, placed in the Agency boarding school, and "reformed" by strict discipline. He said the Dreamer doctrine should be eliminated so that the Indians would join the Agency church. He was finally given his "authority," with the United States Army to back him up.[276]

With all these demands increasing his own burden of responsibility, Chief Joseph realized that he and his people would have to accept and adapt to a new way of life. The increasing influx of the white farmers and the authority of the Army told Chief Joseph only too plainly that his claims on the Wallowa Valley were being overridden. He saw clearly the need for compromise between the Indian and the white culture.[277]

On January 14, 1879, in Washington, DC, Chief Joseph spoke to an assembly of cabinet members, congressmen, and diplomats. He stated, "I can not [sic] understand how the Government sends out a man to fight us, as it did General Miles, and then breaks his word. Such a Government has something wrong about it."[278] His telling of the causes of the war, his people's trials, and their present difficulties was eloquent and moving.

As the years passed, Chief Joseph's efforts finally began to meet with a small success. His persuasive appeals had stirred consciences among people outside the government and had inspired many influential organizations and individuals in the East to take up his cause. Newspapermen and other visitors interviewed Chief Joseph, inspected the Indians' condition, and kept his cause before the public. Chief Joseph's dignity and personal qualities never failed to impress the whites who met him, and the many articles written about him kept letters, telegrams and appeals flowing into Washington. By 1883, Joseph's future was a national issue.[279]

Long before 1883, however, Chief Joseph had impressed a number of people who had come to know much about him.

After the battle of Big Hole on August 9 and 10, 1877, James H. Mills, editor of the Deer Lodge's *The New North-West* said:

> No force, regulars or volunteers, in numbers of less than 300 well-armed fighting men had any business with that Nez Perce band in an open fight. Enthusiasm and courage would doubtless have carried 100 or 150 volunteers into the Nez Perces camp. The result would have been discomfiture and a country full of stricken homes.[280]

While the Nez Perce were fleeing to Canada and the army was chasing them, the soldiers themselves expressed compassion for their plight, particularly those of the Seventh Cavalry and George Armstrong Custer fame. The men of the Seventh Cavalry had joined the campaign later than some of the soldiers who had been in the field all summer. These newer arrivals, therefore, had had opportunity to follow the newspaper articles detailing the chase. Trooper Theodore W. Goldin affirmed that "our sympathies were with the Indians" and admitted that "the resourcefulness of those Indians was the cause of much talk among our men." He also acknowledged that "we felt they had received more than the traditional Double Cross.

We fought them, of course, but our hearts were not in it as in the case of the Siouz [sic], Cheyennes and Apaches."[281] Trooper William C. Slaper thought that "the Nez Perces were a good people and very much abused by our pin-head Government officials."[282]

In the spring of 1885, when 268 men, women, and children remained in the band, the Nez Perce were returned to the Pacific Northwest. In sharp contrast to the fighting retreat on horseback they had made in 1877, this trip was taken by rail.

Chief Joseph never realized his dream of returning to his Wallowa homeland, but "in his efforts to do so, he emerged as an eloquent spokesman for the ideals of liberty, fraternity and equality upon which the Constitution of the United States itself is assumed to rest."[283]

As a dedicated pleader for his people, Chief Joseph, conquered and powerless, was a more impressive figure than he had ever been:

> He towered morally over the whites who came to see him; and when they returned to Washington, they took with them the unforgettable memory of a humanitarian who spoke with the passion and courage of a fighter for freedom, and the wisdom and dignity of a statesman.[284]

Through the years, Chief Joseph did not give up his fight. In June and July of 1900 he succeeded in having his case reheard. During this investigation, Indian Inspector James McLaughlin took Chief Joseph back to the Wallowa Valley. Chief Joseph found his father's grave enclosed by a fence built by a white friend. At the site, Chief Joseph wept. In spite of everything, McLaughlin ruled against the Nez Perce returning to the Wallowa Valley. In 1903 Chief Joseph spoke for his cause in Seattle and, in 1904, the year he died, he pled in Washington, DC, in New York, and at the Saint Louis Exposition.[285]

This seventy-five-day war involved three separate military divisions and brought troops from California, Alaska, and Georgia. Chief Joseph tested the expertise of distinguished Civil War generals. In the end, the war that Howard had brought on by his policy of force cost the United States $1,873,410.43, not including the losses of private individuals. The Nez Perce survivors of the struggle, once a rich and self-sufficient people, were made destitute, and thereafter they became burdens to the American taxpayer. The Indians had lost their horses, cattle, guns, personal possessions, savings of gold dust and cash, homes, freedom—everything but their honor. [286]

Carlos A. Schwantes says:

> The events of mid-1877 cannot actually be described as warfare. Eight hundred Indian men, women and children, including a herd of more than two thousand horses, made a desperate flight across the Bitter Root Mountains to the plains of Montana, where they hoped to find safety among their friends the Crows. Failing that, they planned to seek sanctuary in Canada. Theirs was less a retreat than a flight to safety, a tragic odyssey in which they were pursued by Howard and his soldiers.[287]

During an interview for the North American Review of April 1879, Joseph said:

> Whenever the White man treats the Indian as they treat each other, then we shall have no more wars. We shall be all alike—brothers of one father and one mother, with one sky above us and one country around us, and one government for all. Then the Great Spirit Chief . . . will smile upon this land, and send rain to wash out the bloody spots made by brothers' hands upon the face of the earth. . . . I hope that no more groans of wounded men and women will ever go to the ear of the Great Spirit Chief above, and that all people may be one people.[288] For this time the Indian race is waiting and praying. . . . In-mut-too-yah-lat-lat has spoken for his people.[289]

EPILOGUE

When Indian Inspector James McLaughlin made a final ruling against the Nez Perce ever returning to the Wallowa Valley, Chief Joseph's last hope was shattered. He took to sitting beside his campfire, looking out at the hills before him and murmuring, "*Halo manitah.*" (He would not live to see another winter.)[290] For whole days at a time after that, he remained silent and motionless. Chief Joseph died alone on September 21, 1904, at Nespelem, Washington. Dr. Edward H. Latham, the agency physician (and erstwhile photographer who was so voluble about Joseph's painting-himself-black, picture-taking antics) reported simply that he had died of a broken heart.[291]

* * *

In an article entitled "Nez Perce Go Home Again: Tribe Owns Land Again for First Time since Chief Joseph Forced Out," the Port Angeles, Washington, *Peninsula Daily News* of June 13, 1997 reported:

> For the first time in 120 years, the Nez Perce again own land in Oregon's Wallowa country. The Nez Perce have bought a 10,300-acre cattle ranch . . . from the Bonneville Power Administration. . . . The Chief Joseph Preserve, as the land will be known, will serve mostly as winter range for elk. It is also home to black bear, bighorn sheep, mule deer, peregrine falcons and steelhead.[292]

* * *

Intelligence, dependability in exercising responsibilities, initiative, persistence, adaptability, judgment, and humor are also some of the ingredients Ralph Stogdill lists in his *Handbook of Leadership: A Survey of Theory and Research.*[293]

At the Bear Paw Mountains in Montana on October 5, 1877, Chief Joseph surrendered the remnants of his band—87 men, 184 women, 147 children—to General Oliver Howard and Colonel Nelson Miles with these words:

> Tell General Howard I know his heart. What he told me before I have in my heart. I am tired of fighting. Our chiefs are killed. Looking Glass is dead. Toohoolhoolzote is dead. The old men are all dead. It is the young men who say, "Yes" or "No." He who led the young men is dead. It is cold and we have no blankets. The little children are freezing to death. My people, some of them have run away to the hills, and have no blankets, no food. No one knows where they are—perhaps freezing to death. I want time to look for my children—and see how many of them I can find. Maybe I shall find them among the dead. Hear me my chiefs! I am tired. My heart is sick and sad. From where the sun now stands, I will fight no more forever.[294]

If he had foreseen that after his surrender 120 years would pass before the Nez Perce would be allowed to return home to the Wallowa Valley, would Chief Joseph have gone back in time, if possible, and for his people said, "No surrender, ever"?

By Ralph Stogdill's definition *was* Chief Joseph a "true leader"? Chief Joseph had no acquaintance with either Stogdill or the archetype *Handbook of Leadership: A Survey of Theory and Research.* He merely, instinctively, daily lived his personal code ten decades before Stogdill set some precepts on paper and labeled them "leadership qualities."

In-mut-too-yah-lat-lat has spoken for his people.[295]

ENDNOTES

1. Helen Howard, *Saga of Chief Joseph* (Caldwell, ID: Caxton Printers, 1941), 9.
2. Benjamin Capps, *The Great Chiefs* (Alexandria, VA: Time-Life Books, 1975), 165.
3. Howard, *Saga,* 34.
4. Mary W. Avery, *Washington: A History of the Evergreen State* (Seattle: University of Washington Press, 1965), 193.
5. Benjamin Capps, *The Great Chiefs* (Time Life Education, 1975), 165.
6. Oscar Winther, *The Great Northwest* (New York: Alfred Knopf, 1956), 250.
7. Howard, *Saga,* 23.
8. Avery, *History of the Evergreen State,* 193.
9. Ralph Stogdill, *Handbook of Leadership: A Survey of Theory and Research* (New York: Free Press), 1974.
10. Ibid., vii.
11. Ibid., 143.
12. Ibid., 82.
13. *Funk & Wagnalls New Standard Dictionary of the English Language* (New York and London: Funk & Wagnalls Company, 1938), 1,404.
14. Ibid., 1,405.
15. Stogdill, *Handbook,* 411.
16. G. Adams, *Chief Joseph's Own Story* (Fairfield, WA: Ye Galleon Press, 1973), 11.
17. M. Gidley, *With One Sky Above Us* (New York: G.P. Putnam's Sons, 1979), 74.
18. Alvin Josephy, *Nez Perce Country* (Lincoln: University Nebraska Press, 2007), 102.
19. Merrill Beal, *I Will Fight No More Forever* (Seattle: University of Washington Press, 1963), 278.
20. *Nez Perce Country: A Handbook for the National Park* (Washington, DC: U.S. Department of the Interior, 1983), 133–134.
21. Howard, *Saga,* 16.
22. Ibid., 16.
23. L.V. McWhorter, *Hear Me, My Chiefs!* (Caldwell, ID: Caxton Printers, 1952), 142.
24. F. Haines, *The Nez Perces* (Norman: University of Oklahoma Press, 1955), 227.
25. Howard, *Saga,* 108.
26. Jerome Greene, *Nez Perce Summer 1877* (Helena: Montana Historical Society Press, 2000), 16.
27. Alvin M. Josephy, *The Nez Perce Indians and the Opening of the Northwest* (New Haven: Yale University Press, 1971), 477.
28. Howard, *Saga,* 110–111.
29. Ibid., 129.
30. Ibid., 128.
31. Winther, *Great Northwest,* 177.
32. Ibid., 250.
33. Gidley, *With One Sky,* 73.
34. Howard, *Saga,* 28–29.
35. Ibid., 76.
36. Haines, *The Nez Perces,* 225.
37. Ibid., 225.
38. Beal, *Fight No More,* 36–37.
39. Josephy, *Nez Perce Indians,* 446.
40. M. Brown, *Flight of the Nez Perce* (Lincoln: University of Nebraska Press, 1983), 38.
41. Ibid., 39.

42. Ibid., 39.
43. Haines, *The Nez Perces,* 218.
44. Josephy, *Nez Perce Indians,* 452.
45. Haines, *The Nez Perces,* 232–233.
46. Howard, *Saga,* 37–38.
47. McWhorter, *Hear Me, My Chiefs!,* 147.
48. Howard, *Saga,* 124.
49. Greene, *Nez Perce Summer,* 18.
50 Bill Gulick, *Traveler's History of Washington* (Caldwell, ID: Caxton Printers, 1996), 529.
51. Beal, *Fight No More,* 41.
52. Haines, *The Nez Perces,* 241–242.
53. Bill Gulick, *Chief Joseph Country, Land of the Nez Perce* (Caldwell, ID: Caxton Printers, 1981), 175.
54. Ibid., 175.
55. Frederick J. Dockstader, *Great North American Indians: Profiles in Life and Leadership* (New York: Van Nostrand Reinhold Company, 1977), 130.
56. Beal, *Fight No More,* 41.
57. Howard, *Saga,* 103.
58. Josephy, *Nez Perce Country,* 103.
59. Howard, *Saga,* 106.
60. Ibid., 107.
61. Gulick, *Chief Joseph Country,* 179.
62. Josephy, *Nez Perce Indians,* 472.
63. Ibid., 442–443.
64. Avery, *History of the Evergreen State,* 193.
65. Gulick, *Chief Joseph Country,* 189.
66. M. Gidley, *Kopet: A Documentary Narrative of Chief Joseph's Last Years* (Chicago: Contemporary Books, 1981), 27.
67. Josephy, *Nez Perce Indians,* 494–495.
68. Ibid., 495.
69. Haines, *The Nez Perces,* 234–235.
70. *Nez Perce Country: Handbook,* 152.
71. Josephy, *Nez Perce Indians,* 447.
72. Ibid., 447.
73. Gulick, *Chief Joseph Country,* 185.
74. Josephy, *Nez Perce Indians,* 466–467.
75. Beal, *Fight No More,* 40.
76. Ibid., 41.
77. Greene, *Nez Perce Summer,* 16.
78. Kent Nerburn, *Chief Joseph & the Flight of the Nez Perce* (New York: Harper Collins, 2005), 136.
79. Gulick, *Chief Joseph Country,* 231.
80. Greene, *Nez Perce Summer,* 180.
81. Beal, *Fight No More,* 248.
82. Brown, *Flight of the Nez Perce,* 415.
83. Beal, *Fight No More,* 279.
84. Josephy, *Nez Perce Indians,* 614.
85. Ibid., 611–612.
86. Howard, *Saga,* 356.
87. Ibid., 365.
88. Erskine Wood, *Days with Chief Joseph* (Vancouver, WA: Rose Wind Press, Centennial Edition, 1991), 35.
89. Howard, *Saga,* 212.
90. Gidley, *One Sky,* 73.
91. Adams, *Chief Joseph's Own Story,* 19.
92. Josephy, *Nez Perce Indians,* 496.
93. Raymond Wohlrabe, *The Pacific Northwest* (Cleveland: The World Publishing Company, 1968), 78.
94. Nerburn, *Chief Joseph/Flight,* 91.
95. Howard, *Saga,* 143.
96. Ibid., 143.
97. Avery, *History of the Evergreen State,* 194.
98. Josephy, *Nez Perce Indians,* 508.
99. Gulick, *Chief Joseph Country,* 202.
100. Haines, *The Nez Perces,* 296.
101. Gulick, *Chief Joseph Country,* 206.
102. Wohlrabe, *Pacific Northwest,* 38.
103. Haines, *The Nez Perces,* 262.
104. Howard, *Saga,* 176.
105. Haines, *The Nez Perces,* 261.
106. Gulick, *Chief Joseph Country,* 211.
107. Howard, *Saga,* 203.
108. Ibid., 211–212.
109. Capps, *The Great Chiefs,* 177.
110. Howard, *Saga,* 233.
111. Josephy, *Nez Perce Country,* 126
112. Josephy, *Nez Perce Indians,* 615.
113. Nerburn, *Chief Joseph/Flight,* 134.
114. Beal, *Fight No More,* 142.
115. Greene, *Nez Perce Summer,* 160–161.
116. Gulick, *Chief Joseph Country,* 248–249.
117. Ibid., 249.
118. Ibid., 249.
119. Ibid., 249.
120. Josephy, *Nez Perce Indians,* 580.
121. Howard, *Saga,* 298–299.
122. Haines, *The Nez Perces,* 298.

123. Beal, *Fight No More,* 187.
124. Greene, *Nez Perce Summer,* 224.
125. Ibid., 252.
126. Ibid., 263–264.
127. Nerburn, *Chief Joseph/Flight,* 232.
128. Greene, *Nez Perce Summer,* 266.
129. Howard, *Saga,* 321.
130. Gulick, *Chief Joseph Country,* 264–265.
131. Haines, *The Nez Perces,* 313–314.
132. *Nez Perce Country: Handbook,* 149.
133. Beal, *Fight No More,* 249.
134. Howard, *Saga,* 331.
135. Greene, *Nez Perce Summer,* 312.
136. Haines, *The Nez Perces,* 319.
137. Greene, *Nez Perce Summer,* 312.
138. McWhorter, *Hear Me!,* 517.
139. Ibid., 517–519.
140. Greene, *Nez Perce Summer,* 336.
141. Haines, *The Nez Perces,* 319.
142. Ibid., 333.
143. Nerburn, *Chief Joseph/Flight,* 318.
144. Ibid., 313.
145. Gulick, *Chief Joseph Country,* 275.
146. Gulick, *Traveler's History,* 356.
147. Capps, *The Great Chiefs,* 183.
148. Gulick, *Traveler's History,* 356.
149. Beal, *Fight No More,* 331.
150. Nerburn, *Chief Joseph/Flight,* 371.
151. Howard, *Saga,* 280.
152. Haines, *The Nez Perces,* 244.
153. Josephy, *Nez Perce Indians,* 473.
154. Greene, *Nez Perce Summer,* 18–19.
155. Howard, *Saga,* 273.
156. Ibid., 280.
157. Ibid., 280.
158. Greene, *Nez Perce Summer,* 186.
159. Beal, *Fight No More,* 252.
160. Ibid., 252.
161. Josephy, *Nez Perce Indians,* 607.
162. Howard, *Saga,* 332.
163. Haines, *The Nez Perces,* 318–319.
164. Beal, *Fight No More,* 248.
165. Gidley, *Kopet,* 45.
166. Beal, *Fight No More,* 334.
167. Wood, *Days with Chief Joseph,* 37.
168. Gidley, *With One Sky,* 90–91.
169. Ibid., 114.
170. Ibid., 150.
171. Beal, *Fight No More,* 271.
172. Gulick, *Chief Joseph Country,* 182.
173. Ibid., 182.
174. Ibid., 182.
175. Beal, *Fight No More,* 84.
176. Gulick, *Chief Joseph Country,* 221.
177. Greene, *Nez Perce Summer,* 79.
178. Gulick, *Chief Joseph Country,* 224.
179. Capps, The Great Chiefs, 177.
180. Beal, *Fight No More,* 112.
181. Ibid., 139.
182 Greene, *Nez Perce Summer,* 237.
183. Beal, *Fight No More,* 225.
184. Howard, *Saga,* 309.
185. Beal, *Fight No More,* 225.
186. Howard, *Saga,* 143.
187. Gulick, *Chief Joseph Country,* 170.
188. Brown, *Flight of the Nez Perce,* 116.
189. Haines, *The Nez Perces,* 294.
190. Gulick, *Chief Joseph Country,* 238–239.
191. Howard, *Saga,* 259–260.
192. Ibid., 260.
193. Beal, *Fight No More,* 144–145.
194. Greene, *Nez Perce Summer,* 232.
195. Howard, *Saga,* 312.
196. Brown, *Flight of the Nez Perce,* 415.
197. Howard, *Saga,* 334.
198. Beal, *Fight No More,* p.257.
199. Ibid., 256.
200. Ibid., 256.
201. Ibid., 307.
202. Ibid., 307.
203. Brown, *Flight of the Nez Perce,* 415.
204. Howard, *Saga,* 143.
205. Brown, *Flight of the Nez Perce,* 116–117.
206. Ibid., 117.
207. Greene, *Nez Perce Summer,* 54.
208. Ibid., 54–58.
209. Brown, *Flight of the Nez Perce,* 415.
210. Beal, *Fight No More,* 70.
211. Capps, *The Great Chiefs,* 180.
212. Howard, *Saga,* 359.
213. Ibid., 359–360.
214. Ibid., 360.
215. Beal, *Fight No More,* 215–216.
216. Ibid., 215.
217. Brown, *Flight of the Nez Perce,* 266.
218. Greene, *Nez Perce Summer,* 242.
219. Howard, *Saga,* 329.

220. Beal, *Fight No More,* 257.
221. Gulick, *Chief Joseph Country,* 269.
222. Haines, *The Nez Perces,* 315.
223. Ibid., 315.
224. Greene, *Nez Perce Summer,* 313.
225. Ibid., 312.
226. Ibid., 312.
227. Beal, *Fight No More,* 253.
228. Ibid., 256.
229. Ibid., 309.
230. A. and J. Salisbury, *Here Rolled the Covered Wagons* (Seattle: Superior Publishing, 1948), 126.
231. Wood, *Days with Chief Joseph,* 35.
232. Howard, *Saga,* 358.
233. Ibid., 366.
234. Gidley, *With One Sky,* 115–117.
235. Howard, *Saga,* 83.
236. Wood, *Days with Chief Joseph,* 36.
237. Beal, *Fight No More,* 247.
238. Howard, *Saga,* 323–324.
239. Greene, *Nez Perce Summer,* 296–297.
240. Gulick, *Chief Joseph Country,* 267.
241. Winther, Great Northwest, 252.
242. Greene, *Nez Perce Summer,* 297– 298.
243. Ibid., 299.
244. Ibid., 300–301.
245. Ibid., 298.
246. S. Warren, *The Farthest Frontier* (New York: MacMillan, 1949), 27.
247. Gulick, *Chief Joseph Country,* 276.
248. Warren, *Farthest Frontier,* 27.
249. Josephy, *Nez Perce Indians,* 622.
250. Gidley, *With One Sky,* 73–74.
251. Josephy, *Nez Perce Country,* 147.
252. Gulick, *Chief Joseph Country,* 293.
253. Josephy, *Nez Perce Country,* 148.
254. Gidley, *Kopet,* 36.
255. Ibid., 37.
256. Ibid., 38.
257. Ibid., 39.
258. Jalmar, Johnson, *Builders of the Northwest* (Binghampton, NY: Vail-Ballou Press, 1963), 208.
259. Howard, *Saga,* 371.
260. Wood, *Days with Chief Joseph,* vi.
261. Greene, *Nez Perce Summer,* 322.
262. Ibid., 323–324.
263. R. Kirk, and C. Alexander, *Exploring Washington's Past* (Seattle: University of Washington Press, 1990), 65.
264. Beal, *Fight No More,* 280.
265. Josephy, *Nez Perce Country,* 102.
266. Dockstader, *Great North American Indians,* 128.
267. Gidley, *With One Sky,* 74.
268. Haines, *The Nez Perces,* 234.
269. Ibid., 234.
270. Gulick, *Chief Joseph Country,* 183.
271. Ibid., 184.
272. Haines, *The Nez Perces,* 236–237.
273. Ibid., 328.
274. Greene, *Nez Perce Summer,* 336.
275. Ibid., 344–345.
276. Haines, *The Nez Perces,* 230.
277. Ibid., 233.
278. Warren, *Farthest Frontier,* 27.
279. *Nez Perce Country: Handbook,* 155.
280. Brown, *Flight,* 280.
281. Greene, *Nez Perce Summer,* 227–228.
282. Ibid., 228.
283. Gidley, *With One Sky,* 73.
284. Josephy, *Nez Perce Indians,* 620.
285. Gidley, *With One Sky,* 74.
286. Josephy, *Nez Perce Indians,* 613.
287. Schwantes, Carlos, *The Pacific Northwest* (University of Nebraska Press, 1989), 120–121.
288. Salisbury, *Rolled Covered Wagons,* 126.
289. Howard, *Saga,* 351.
290. Ibid., 367.
291. Gidley, *One Sky,* 14.
292. Associated Press, "Nez Perce Go Home Again. Tribe Owns Land Again . . . Since Chief Joseph Forced Out," *Peninsula Daily News,* June 13, 1997, A-8.
293. Stogdill, *Handbook,* 62.
294. Josephy, *Nez Perce Indians,* 609.
295. Gidley, *With One Sky,* 74.

BIBLIOGRAPHY

Associated Press. "Nez Perce Go Home Again. Tribe Owns Land Again for First Time Since Chief Joseph Forced Out." *Peninsula Daily News,* Port Angeles, WA, June 13, 1997.

Avery, Mary W. *Washington: A History of the Evergreen State.* Seattle: University of Washington Press, 1965.

Beal, Merrill D. *I Will Fight No More Forever. Chief Joseph and the Nez Perce War.* Seattle: University of Washington Press, 1963.

Brown, Mark H. *The Flight of the Nez Perce.* New York: G.P. Putnam's Sons, 1967.

Capps, Benjamin. *The Great Chiefs.* Alexandria, VA: Time-Life Books, 1975.

Dockstader, Frederick J. *Great North American Indians: Profiles in Life and Leadership.* New York: Van Nostrand Reinhold Company, 1977.

Funk & Wagnalls New Standard Dictionary of the English Language. New York and London: Funk & Wagnalls Company, 1938.

Gidley, M. *Kopet: A Documentary Narrative of Chief Joseph's Last Years.* Chicago: Contemporary Books, 1981.

Gidley, M. *With One Sky Above Us: Life on an American Indian Reservation at the Turn of the Century.* Leicester, UK. Windward, 1979.

Greene, Jerome A. *Nez Perce Summer 1877, The U.S. Army and the Nee-Me-Poo Crisis.* Helena: Montana Historical Society Press, 2000.

Gulick, Bill. *Chief Joseph Country, Land of the Nez Perce.* Caldwell, ID: Caxton Printers, 1994.

Gulick, Bill. *Traveler's History of Washington, A.* Caldwell, ID: Caxton Printers, 1996.

Haines, Francis. *The Nez Perces, Tribesmen of the Columbia Plateau.* Norman: University of Oklahoma Press, 1955.

Howard, Helen Addison. *Saga of Chief Joseph.* Caldwell, ID: Caxton Printers, 1941.

Johnson, Jalmar. *Builders of the Northwest.* Binghampton, NY: Vail-Ballou Press, 1963.

Josephy, Alvin M., Jr. *Nez Perce Country.* Lincoln: University of Nebraska Press, 2007.

Josephy, Alvin M., Jr. *The Nez Perce Indians and the Opening of the Northwest.* New Haven: Yale University Press, 1971.

Kirk, Ruth and Alexander, Carmela. *Exploring Washington's Past, a Road Guide to History.* Seattle: University of Washington Press, 1990.

McWhorter, L. V. *Hear Me, My Chiefs! Nez Perce Legend & History.* Caldwell, ID: Caxton Printers, 2001.

Nerburn, Kent. *Chief Joseph & the Flight of the Nez Perce.* New York: Harper Collins Publishers, 2005.

Nez Perce Country: A Handbook for the National Park. Washington, DC: U.S. Department of the Interior, 1983.

Salisbury, Albert and Jane. *Here Rolled the Covered Wagons.* New York: Bonanza Books, 1948.

Schwantes, Carlos. *The Pacific Northwest, An Interpretive History.* Lincoln: University of Nebraska Press, 1989.

Stogdill, Ralph M. *Handbook of Leadership, A Survey of Theory and Research.* New York: Free Press, 1974.

Warren, Sydney. *Farthest Frontier, The Pacific Northwest.* New York: MacMillan Company, 1949.

Winther, Oscar. *The Great Northwest.* New York: Alfred Knopf, 1948.

Wohlrabe, Raymond. *The Pacific Northwest.* Cleveland: The World Publishing Company, 1968.

Wood, Erskine. *Days With Chief Joseph.* Vancouver, WA: Rose Wind Press, Centennial Edition, 1991.

Ye Galleon Press. *Chief Joseph's Own Story.* Fairfield, WA: Ye Galleon Press, 1973.

ABOUT THE AUTHOR

Louise Lenahan Wallace received a BA from Western Washington University and is the author of five novels and numerous stories in magazines and anthologies. She has received writing awards from Pacific Northwest Writers Association, Wyoming Writers, and San Mateo Fair's Literary contests.

In addition to writing, Louise has served as the public relations representative for the Cancer Society's local chapter, as well as the secretary for her square dance club. She is the mother of two daughters and lives in Washington state.